A Child at a Time

A Child at a Time

Understanding Temperament

LORAINE D. COOK

The University of the West Indies Press
Mona • St Augustine • Cave Hill • Global • Five Islands

The University of the West Indies Press
7A Gibraltar Hall Road, Mona
Kingston 7, Jamaica
www.uwipress.com

© 2024, Loraine D. Cook

All rights reserved. Published 2024

A catalogue record of this book is available from the National Library of Jamaica.

ISBN: 978-976-640-931-9 (print)
ISBN: 978-976-640-947-0 (epub)

The University of the West Indies Press has no responsibility for the persistence or accuracy of URLs for external or third-party internet websites referred to in this publication and does not guarantee that any content on such websites is, or will remain, accurate or appropriate.

Cover and text design by Christina Moore Fuller
Cover painting by David Christopher Cook
Printed in the United States of America

DEDICATION

I dedicate this book to David Christopher Cook. As my husband, he is my inspiration and rock. David is always available to discuss my ideas. I thank him for his patience, love and commitment.

Contents

List of Figures ... ix
List of Tables ... xi
Preface ... xiii
Acknowledgements ... xv
Introduction ... xvii
Defining Acronyms ... xxi

1. Temperamental Differences ... 1
2. Understanding Parents' Interactions with Their Children ... 22
3. School Factors and Temperament ... 38
4. Fostering Development of Jamaican Children ... 51
5. Teachers' Assessment of a Sample of Jamaican Children's Temperament ... 73
6. INSIGHTS into Children's Temperament Programme ... 88
7. The Influence of INSIGHTS on Parenting Practice ... 97
8. The Influence of INSIGHTS on Teaching Practices ... 117
9. Facilitating Differences in Children's Development ... 145

References ... 161
Index ... 179

List of Figures

Figure 1.1:	Hypothetical Relation between Environmental Stress and Behaviour Problems as Mediated by Predispositional Risk	... 19
Figure 7.1:	How often did parents use what they learnt from INSIGHTS?	... 101
Figure 7.2:	How much did parents learn?	... 102
Figure 7.3:	How useful did parents find the information received?	... 102
Figure 7.4:	How did the parents rate the facilitators?	... 103
Figure 7.5:	Parents Words That Describe How They Found the INSIGHTS Experience	... 113
Figure 8.1:	How often did teachers use what they learnt in INSIGHTS?	... 122
Figure 8.2:	How much did teachers learn?	... 122
Figure 8.3:	How useful was the new information teachers received?	... 123
Figure 8.4:	How effective was the teachers' facilitators?	... 123
Figure 9.1:	INSIGHTS Wall in Alpha School	... 148

List of Tables

Table 1.1:   Higher-Order Behavioural Tendencies   ...   13

Table 2.1:   Summary of Episodes of the Strange Situation   ...   24

Table 5.1:   Means, SDs, and Cronbach's Alpha of the T-SATI Dimensions   ...   85

Preface

As adults, we are responsible for nurturing and shaping the lives of young children. We are responsible for shaping these lives into healthy functioning adults and citizens of our society.

While nurturing children, it is important that we, as adults, do not take on the role of filling up empty jars; children are not blank slates for us adults to scribble all over. Instead, they are born with DNAs that hold all their inherent characteristics that unfold as they grow and mature. Psychological traits from mental illness to mental abilities characterize some families. DNA can be used to detect mental illness from birth "long before any brain or behavioural markers can be detected" (Plomin 2018, 6). Similarly, certain individuals' characteristics, in other words, temperaments, have been linked to their DNA (Kagan and Snidman 2004). Children are born with biological features to understand their environment from birth.

Consequently, as their guides, we adults must understand their inherent pathways. It is imperative that children are given room to express their wants, emotions, and actions, and we need to understand these expressions. We need not embrace their ways as always right, but we should regulate our irritation and disappointment when we see their waywardness. These waywardnesses are opportunities for us adults to grow to understand and prize children's differences, appreciate the fact that they are different from us, and nurture those differences (Keirsey and Bates 1984).

Differences in children's temperament impact various aspects of their life experiences from childhood through adolescence and throughout their adult lives. In a longitudinal study, individual differences in behaviour were observed at age three. These behavioural differences have, for example, been "linked to adult mental illness, number of years of educational attainment, number of adjudicated criminal offences, marital discord and divorce, and income levels" (Martin, Lease and Slobodskaya 2020, 4).

This book introduces the role of children's temperament (that is, the individual's characteristics), parents, teachers and peers in influencing the behaviour or action of children in particular in the classroom. I hope this book will help adults, specifically classroom teachers, responsible for the development of children (birth to eight years) to make sense of children's disruptive behaviours, otherwise referred to as problem behaviours. Sometimes, students' sense of indignation and outrage may be a reaction to their environment; most times, they react to the negative environment they are situated in at home, on the playfield or in the classroom. For some students, it is the lack of understanding of how to control the negative reactions of their temperament that causes a consistent display of disruptive behaviours. Many of these children with problem behaviours have few friends or are from homes pierced with the knife of poverty. Students' behaviour at school may mirror their relationship with parents and other family members at home; it may be a cry for help. I hope that the information in this publication will bring understanding and care for children by adults. Our role as adults is to help children manage the negative reaction of their temperament, not to treat them with disdain nor as evildoers; they are our adults of tomorrow.

Acknowledgements

I am grateful to:
- Culture, Health, Arts, Sports, and Education Fund (CHASE) for their financial support for the intervention for three years (2014–17).
- Professor Sandee McClowry for unselfishly sharing and guiding the implementation of the intervention in Jamaica.
- Mrs Grace McLean, the then CEO of the Ministry of Education, for her support of the programme and its implementation in the early childhood institutions.
- Dr Rose Davies, senior lecturer at the School of Education, for the commitment and drive that she brought to the project. Dr Rose Davies also chaired the project advisory committee for the duration of the project.
- The advisory committee members who ensured that the project was monitored and managed efficiently: Pastor Bruce Fletcher, Dr Mariette Newman, Mr Collins, and Mrs Gayle Mitchell.
- Professors Jennings-Craig and Stafford Griffith, directors of the School of Education, who in their separate terms gave their support.
- Early Childhood Commission (ECC) for their commitment and dedication through the involvement of

their development officers in the first two and half years of the project. The development officers were the first facilitators of INSIGHTS in the various schools, both in the urban and rural areas.

- Mrs Michelle Campbell from ECC, whose commitment and drive enabled the collaboration between School of Education and ECC. Mrs Nicolette McDonnough Foster, principal of Alpha Infant School, whose commitment and support added passion to implementing the INSIGHTS programme.
- The development officers who embraced the principles of the programme and added passion and professionalism in the delivery of the programme.
- To all the principals, teachers and parents who strive for the improvement and betterment of Jamaica's children, we are forever grateful.

Thanks to the following family and friends who were a tremendous encouragement:

- My husband, David Cook, for his unrelenting support.
- My sons, Christopher, Jonathan and Luke Cook.
- My sister, Carol Palmer.
- My grandson, Ezra.
- I am grateful for the wisdom and advice of Dr Tony Bastick, Professor Beatrice Boufoy Bastick, Prof. Errol Miller and the late Dr Monica and Earl Brown.
- My friends and affirmers, Dicky Powell, Charlton Romer, Alison Nicholson, Bruce Fletcher, Ansel Aiken and Rawle Tyson.
- My mother, Mrs Listene Victoria Palmer, has left an indelible mark on my life.

Finally, I express gratitude to the Fulbright Scholarship Programme of the US Embassy, which facilitated this collaborative activity between the School of Education, University of the West Indies and New York University.

Introduction

Children between the ages of three and eight in the classroom have diverse characteristics (temperament); teachers and parents influence these children. However, these adults in a school setting have a common goal – helping children be educated and thereby preparing them to be healthy citizens of society. Teachers and parents who have successfully educated children always provide an environment that encourages learning and development. For the most part, this environment emphasizes the psychological dimension – providing emotional support and maintaining a safe environment for children to explore; that is, providing a threat-free environment. I am a teacher-educator who is passionate about children from birth being understood through the creation of a loving and nurturing environment. As adults, we want to be understood, so it is expedient that parents and teachers from very early in children's life endeavour to understand each child. It is important to respond and communicate with them in such a way that the child can develop a healthy self-perception and thereby be able to relate to others.

Both teachers and parents are significant others in children's lives and therefore are responsible for providing a loving and nurturing environment for children to develop. In so doing, it is important for adults to understand the characteristics of the children they are responsible for and how their response and reactions affect children and their subsequent development. While this book targets educators, parents can also benefit from the information and policymakers/planners for the early childhood years. Understanding children's temperament is critical because children "pay an exorbitant price" when disciplined by adults who do not understand their characteristics (Levine 2002).

There are eight chapters: The first three chapters provide general information on temperamental differences and the different temperaments interaction with parental and school factors during children's early development:

In chapter 1, we discussed temperamental differences and the rationale for studying temperament, assessed the stability of temperament over time and focused on a theoretical discussion of the interactions between temperament and the environment.

The focus of chapter 2 is on the interactions between parental factors and children's temperament. First, there is a brief discussion of the interaction between attachment and temperament. Then, we look at different child-rearing styles and their interactions with children's temperaments.

In chapter 3, we focused on school factors and temperament. First, we discuss the teacher-student relationship and how the relationship is influenced by students' characteristics (temperament).

In chapter 4, we discussed the behavioural management strategies used in the development process of Jamaican children. The chapter included a discussion of the early childhood landscape in Jamaica. In discussing the early childhood landscape, we described several interventions and programmes targeting children in the Jamaican context. The chapter ends with an expanded discussion of the INSIGHTS into Children Temperament Programme.

Chapter 5 aims to discuss in more detail the various dimensions of temperament and their implication for teachers' classroom practices. The discussion includes the temperamental profile of what typical children could look like based on a sample of Jamaican children's temperament profiles reported by teachers.

Chapters 6–9 focus on the INSIGHTS into Children Programme. Chapter 6 gives background information on INSIGHTS in the Jamaican context (reports on the preliminary as a preliminary phase in the pilot of the programme in Jamaica. Chapter 7 reports on Jamaican parents' view of INSIGHTS following their participation in the programme; chapter eight reports on Jamaican teachers' view of INSIGHTS following their participation in the programme, and chapter nine, in this concluding chapter, activities of a selected school are shared as an example of sustainability of the INSIGHTS programme in Jamaican schools.

A Child at a Time is a call to educators, parents and possible policymakers to recognize that children's differences should not be taken for granted, especially in the early stages of their development. The book emphasizes differences in children's characters and socio-emotional needs and how these differences influence how children respond to teachers' and parents' behavioural management strategies.

Defining Acronyms

DNA	–	"deoxyribonucleic acid, is the hereditary material in humans and almost all other organisms" (Source: https://www.genome.gov/genetics-glossary/Deoxyribonucleic-Acid)
CEO	–	Chief Executive Officer
CHASE Fund	–	Culture, Health, Arts, Sports and Education Fund
ECC	–	Early Childhood Commission
DRD4	–	"DRD4 (Dopamine Receptor D4) is a Protein Coding gene. Diseases associated with DRD4 include Attention Deficit-Hyperactivity Disorder and Autonomic Nervous System Disease" (Source: https://www.ncbi.nlm.nih.gov/gene/1815)
DC	–	Development Officers
SU	–	Surgency extraversion
EC	–	Effortful Control
CE	–	Centre for Early Childhood Education
CAPRI	–	The Caribbean Policy Research Institute
NYU	–	New York University
PALS	–	Peace and Love in Schools
PDR	–	Parental Daily Report
PECE	–	Project for Early Childhood Education
T-SATI	–	Teacher School-Age Temperament Inventory)
UWI	–	The University of the West Indies

1. Temperamental Differences

> Two children may dress themselves or ride a bicycle with the same dexterity and have similar motives for engaging in these activities. Two adolescents may display similar learning abilities and intellectual interests, and their academic performances may coincide. These actions reflect their motivations and abilities. Yet, these two children or adolescents may differ significantly with regards to the quickness with which they move, the ease with which they enter a new social situation and the effort required by others to distract them from their chosen activity. These variations reflect differences in temperament (Chess 1990, 314–15).

From the moment of conception, the structure is laid for individual differences in behaviour. Even before babies are born, mothers observe that some babies are more physically active than others; some poke and kick from within the womb, while others seldom move (Martin, Lease and Slobodskaya 2020). Once babies are born, we observe differences in their behaviour; some babies adapt to a new environment more easily, while others are more physically active. By the time children enter the preschool stage and progress through the school system, parents and teachers notice the differences in behaviours and reactions. Some are withdrawn when meeting strangers, while others are excited and easily interact with strangers. Some children constantly run and jump, while others sit quietly for extended periods. Researchers have sought to study these differences in behaviour to address questions such as how are these behaviours predictive of individuals' future behaviours? How stable are these early patterns of behaviour throughout an individual's life? What causes these behavioural patterns in children?

In response to the latter question, psychologists and researchers from different professional disciplines and fields have provided evidence that the influences are multifaceted. The influences are a mixture of biology and the environment. Concerning genes, Plomin (2018) noted that in the 1960s, scientists conducted long-term studies with twins and adoptees that provided evidence that genetics contributed to the psychological differences between us. Fifty per cent of our psychological differences, according to Plomin, is caused by genetics. In other words, at the core of who we are and what distinguishes each of us is our DNA, genetics. Deater-Deckard and Wang (2012) argue that behavioural scientists have clear evidence that genetics contribute to individual differences in anger and irritability. Scientists have identified that an individual's tendency to express anger is associated with the D4 receptor (DRD4) (Martin, Lease and Slobodskaya, 2020). Genetics only partially explain a child's behaviour; the child's environment also interacts with genetics to produce the displayed patterns of behaviours. The environment exerts influences on the child's genetic expression. One perspective on the interaction between genetics and the environment is that "parents create environments for themselves that tend to foster the same genetic tendencies in their children" (165).

Children's differences in behavioural and emotional responses to difficult or new situations in infancy are postulated to be biologically based. Hence there is a degree of stability in their characteristics, namely, their temperament, as they mature through the developmental life span (Blandon et al. 2010). However, add to the genetic base of a child's temperament, there are changes in the child's temperament that are likely to occur biologically as the brain matures and as the environment and child adjust to the maturation stages – transitioning from the family system to the school system.

Children's temperament, patterns of behaviours and emotional responses shape their interactions with the environment. Children's temperamental profiles are determined by how they respond to their environment, and their temperament shapes the reactions they evoke from the environment (Blandon et al. 2010, 1). For example, children who express high levels of negative emotional reaction may experience rejection from their peers; such experiences can accelerate negative reactions, which leads to relationship problems, and children with high levels of negative reaction experience social problems. This chapter gives an overview of temperament. The chapter begins with defining temperament and offers reasons why adults need to understand temperament. Next, the continuity of behaviour styles (temperaments) from infancy to adulthood is examined, citing several longitudinal studies – the chapter ends with a discussion concerning the nature/nurture features of temperament.

Temperament Defined

Temperament represents the early development of personality. Temperament is the early appearance of children's emotional reactions and behaviour styles, consistent across events and situations. Temperament combined with experiences evolve into personality. The process includes the child developing awareness about self, others, and the physical and social world (Rothbart 2007). Self-awareness involves knowing their values (a moral consciousness of what is right or wrong), attitudes (what they like and don't like) and how they cope or deal with certain issues emotionally (Rothbart 2007; Doring 2010). An adult personality includes temperament and more, "particularly the content of thought, skills, habits, values, defences, morals, beliefs, and social cognition" (Rothbart and Bates 2006,

100). Social cognition is the way people remember, process their memories and use the information in social interactions to predict and explain their own actions and that of others (Bulgarelli and Molina 2016).

Why Consider Temperament?

Keogh (2003) and McClowry (2014) offer the following reasons why educators, parents and other caregivers need to consider temperament:

- Temperament describes the behavioural styles of others that contribute to understanding personal and social interactions. In other words, understanding the temperament of individuals helps a teacher or parent to predict behaviours and how the nature of the child's experiences will be affected. For example, "an approaching friendly and active child is likely to seek out new situations, whereas a withdrawing, timid child will avoid them" (Keogh 2003, 3). High energy and active children may put themselves in risky situations that the withdrawn and cautious child may never experience.

- Temperament affects the adult-child interactions – the child's behaviour influences the adult's response or reaction. According to Keogh, "parents of highly active intense, fearless toddlers may have to make special arrangements in their home to ensure a child's safety and teachers may have to give social attention to slow-to-warm-up students who tend to be overlooked in the classroom" (3). Temperament contributes significantly to how individuals remember and interpret situations. Two people can differ in their reporting of the same event; "two students may describe an incident that occurred in the classroom and sound as if they had very different experiences" (McClowry 2014, 7).

- Individuals with a difficult temperament tend to elicit negative reactions from their peers and even parents and teachers, who tend to be more punitive to such children than to those with an easy temperament (Keogh 2003). Temperament is easily recognized in a situation that involves stress or change (McClowry 2014, 7). Stams, Juffer and van Ijzendoorm (2002) in a longitudinal study with one hundred and forty adopted children reported that "an easy temperament was associated with higher levels of social, cognitive, and personality development and fewer behavior problems" (806).

Tracing Temperament from Newborns

Temperamental characteristics are evident as early as in newborns (Kagan and Snidman 2004; Rothbart 2007). Newborns show temperaments such as anxiety and avoidant movement, and by two to three months, infants react by smiling, laughing, and body movements. Anger or distress was observed in infants two to three months old, and fear in the form of behavioural inhibition can be observed by seven to ten months (Rothbart 2007). Kagan and Snidman (2004) conducted a series of experiments with infants that support the early identification of temperamental differences in infants. Howbeit, Rothbart's ages of the infants differ somewhat when various behaviour styles appear. Kagan and Snidman provide an example of how the experiments were carried out with infants. They conducted a longitudinal study on temperament development, focusing on children from the age of four months to eleven years. This study initially involved five hundred infants who were first assessed at four months. Kagan and Snidman described the study: "Initially, the mother looked down at her infant, smiling but not talking, for one minute. She then went to a chair behind the infant to be outside his field of vision. The examiner placed a speaker baffle to the right of the infant and turned on a tape recording that played eight short sentences read by female voices" (15).

The researchers reported that most infants were very quiet and alert during the various experimental situations, while others began "to thrash their arms and legs, and a small number cried" (15).

Following the above, other situations were created by Kagan and Snidman. This second series of experimental situations are described as follows:

> The speaker baffle was removed and the examiner, standing in the back of the infant, presented a set of mobiles composed of one, three, or seven, unfamiliar, colorful toys that moved back and forth in front of the infant's face for nine 20-second trials. Most infants were more active in response to the mobiles than to the taped sentences; some became increasingly aroused over the nine trials, as reflected in vigorous limb movements, and crying. The examiner then dipped a cotton swab into very dilute butyl alcohol and presented it close to the infant's nostrils for eight trials (water was used for the first and last trials, instead of alcohol). The speaker baffle was replaced, and the infant heard a female voice speaking three nonsense syllables (*ma, pa, ga*) at three different loudness levels. (5)

Again, Kagan and Snidman reported that most of the infants were not disturbed by the situations. However, they were able to classify the infants into four groups:

- Twenty per cent of the infants "thrashed and cried, vigorous pumping of the legs and arms, sometimes with arching of the back, on at least 40 percent of the trials" (13). Once the situations were removed, the infants stopped their motor activity and crying. These infants were labelled as high reactive.

- Forty per cent of the infants who exhibited very low motor activity and very low disturbance were labelled as low reactive. Occasionally, these infants with low reactivity would cry and did minimal movements.

- Another 20 per cent showed a low level of movement but were irritable throughout the situations. These infants were labelled as distressed.

- Yet another 10 per cent were highly energetic; this was demonstrated by the pumping of both arms and legs, but no arching of the back and they rarely cried; they were labelled as aroused; and 5 per cent of the infants, the researchers were unable to classify.

At this stage of their study, Kagan and Snidman identified infants with the following temperaments: high active, low active, distressed and aroused. These four groups of infants were followed by the researchers for the next ten to twelve years.

Three hundred of the five hundred were reassessed at fourteen to twenty-one months, and again at thirty-one months. The researchers coded the infants' reaction to the situations of an unfamiliar woman dressed in a white laboratory coat wearing a gas mask and carrying a radio-controlled robot. The children who were previously classified as high reactive were most fearful, those classified as low reactive were least fearful and the other group was not like any of the groups mentioned earlier and was given an average fear score. At the end of these sessions, Kagan and Snidman noted, "these findings convinced us that a temperamental bias contributed to the variation in reactivity at four months and the subsequent tendency to approach or avoid unfamiliar incentives in the second year" (15).

One hundred and ninety-three of the five hundred infants returned to the lab when they were four and a half years of age for two sessions. The researchers concluded, "by contrast, 46 percent of those who had been high-reactive infants were shy, quiet, and timid, compared with only 10 percent of those who had been low-reactive infants" (15). After examining the children again at seven years and eleven years, the researchers wrote: "More high-reactives preserved a serious, non-smiling facial expression at every assessment, from 14 months to 11 years. More low-reactives smiled and frequently laughed at every age. Many low-reactives, but very few high-reactives, smiled and laughed within the first minute of entering the laboratory at 11 years of age" (19).

The researchers found that, on a self-report instrument, the children who were categorized as low-reactives were more likely to report that they were "happy most of the time". Kagan and Snidman also found that the level of fear in response to unfamiliar events during their second year did not predict their behaviour at eleven years. They also assessed the biological changes in the children and noted that low-reactive infants had distinct biological changes by the time they were eleven years. The researchers stated that infants' behaviour at four months was a better predictor of their behaviour at age eleven than variation in fear at one and two years of age. Kagan and Snidman noted that one-fourth of the eleven-year-olds who were shy, quiet and subdued were categorized at four months as high-reactive (as described by their parents at the time). In other words, very few high-reactives were "exuberant, sociable, minimally aroused" eleven-year-olds. A fourth of the low-reactives preserved their expected behaviour. In other words, very few low-reactives became fearful and quiet introverts. Kagan and Snidman concluded that the environment in which the children grew up "can create different personas in those who began life with the same temperamental bias" (24). Thus, supporting the importance of the interaction of nature and nurture in children's development, heredity and children's environment jointly contribute to the evolution of their temperament. This modification in children's behaviours between infancy and the preadolescence stage were also reported by Chess (1990) as infants grew into middle childhood and adolescence, their behaviour style changed somewhat – the boisterous babies who we expect to become energetic adults become the opposite, shy and withdrawn. The low-reactive child we expect to become shy and withdrawn adults become sociable. The expected continuities in children's temperaments were not always the case because of the changes that young adults experience with different activities and persons. We must always be aware that a child's temperament or behaviour style can vary as the child matures because of the influence of caregivers' actions and attitudes. Chess (1990) reported that her research team found that adolescents sought out congenial environments, instead of remaining true to their temperamental characteristics. For some individuals, this quest for change may be internal due to "developmental changes in cognition, physical abilities, and motivation" (320). In other cases, it may be that change is triggered by external factors, such as the family, places and circumstances.

Blandon et al. (2010) concluded from their study that children's temperamental reactivity could be dynamic and change during early childhood. Some children have been found to display the same general behaviour patterns from childhood to adolescence, and some shows changes in their behaviour patterns as they mature. What causes this stability or variability in children's temperament as they grow and mature? Blandon et al. stated that "as children enter new developmental contexts and learn the rules for appropriate emotional behaviour across different situations, they are more equipped to respond to challenging and exciting situations" (13). This supports the notion that children's temperament is not so "hard-wired" that they cannot modify their behaviour. Studies are not conclusive on the continuities of behaviour styles across time into adulthood, whether there are two groups of persons, the ones who change their temperament as they develop (the changers), or the group whose temperament remains stable over time (the constants) (Chess 1990). As noted above by Kagan and Snidman (2004) and Chess (1990), some aspects of temperament do change as individuals mature into adults.

Stability of Temperament

Temperament is at the core of children's psychological function; as a result, researchers have used several ways of assessing children's temperament. Children's behaviour styles continue to be assessed using information from parents through interviews and questionnaires, and observations of children by researchers. Researchers observe children at home or in a laboratory. Subsequent to several investigations, researchers agree that, for the most part, children's temperament develops with age (Berk 2014). As children move through the life span from infant to three years, they are better able to regulate their emotions and attention. In addition to examining children's temperament from infancy, some investigators examine temperament stability over time, starting when children are three years of age – for example, Caspi and Silva (1995).

Caspi and Silva studied a large sample (n=800) of children from the age of three to eighteen years and traced if their early childhood behaviour styles were related to young adulthood. The researchers identified five types of temperaments among children who were three years of age: uncontrollable, inhibited, confident, reserved and well-adjusted. Uncontrollable children were those who scored on the following dimensions: irritability and distractibility. The second type of temperament was the inhibited; the dimensions are shy, fearful, little verbal communication and upset by strangers. The third type of temperament was confident. The dimensions of a confident temperament are willingness and eagerness to tackle and explore the tasks presented to them, not agitated when leaving their parents, good interpersonal skills and adjusted well to new circumstances.

The fourth type of temperament was the reserved; the dimensions are shy, fearful and self-critical. These dimensions are similar to the inhibited temperament but different in that these persons are task-oriented, and their attention-holding capacities are intact, despite some timidity. The fifth and last type of temperament was the well-adjusted. Children in this group knew how to judge situations and were capable of being reserved and controlled when the situation demanded a certain response. Also, they were self-confident and tried to cope with challenging tasks and were initially cautious in situations, but can adjust and become comfortable.

The participating group was reassessed at eighteen years of age. The researchers reported that there were continuities across time. Caspi and Silva concluded: "undercontrolled children scored high on measures of impulsivity, danger seeking, aggression, and interpersonal alienation; inhibited children scored low on measures of impulsivity, danger seeking, aggression, and social potency; confident children scored high on impulsivity; reserved children scored low on social potency; and well-adjusted children continued to exhibit normative behaviours" (486).

Similarly, to Kagan and Snidman, Caspi and Silvia's study gives some support to the stability of individuals temperament from infancy to adolescence. Hence children who were shy and withdrawn when young were low on activity and less likely to seek out new experiences and new situations in adolescence.

What behavioural traits indicate children's competence to adapt easily to school, peers and family and the varying situation within each of the contexts represented? Parents' and educators' awareness of such characteristics can help these adults to assess the children within their care, plan and prepare to help the children who lack the competencies to assimilate into their new environment and thus manage the children's behaviour in ways that are satisfying and productive (Rodd 1996). Martin, Lease and Slobodskaya (2020) reported on several research studies that identified those behavioural patterns parents believe to be most critical in children's ease of adaption to the various types of environments. In conducting these studies, "parents were asked to provide a brief description of their child" (13). The researchers collected forty thousand descriptors from eight countries. These narratives were analysed and yielded fifteen behavioural traits:

Intelligence: Intelligence is perceived by parents as their children's aptitude and speed to learn new academic concepts and skills.

Openness to Experience/Curiosity: Display interest in many different things and are open to new ideas.

Achievement Motivation: Motivation to improve academic skills and knowledge. There is a purpose to meet "demands of the culture for school achievement" (Martin, Lease and Slobodskaya 2020, 15).

Positive Emotionality: Easy to be with and relate; express contentment, joy and happiness that enhances the mood of others; warm and friendly.

Consideration-of-Others: Generous, thoughtful, loving and empathic toward others.

Activity Level: These children have a high-energy level. They run rather than walk. High-energy children liked to participate in sports.

Negative Emotionality: These children tend to exhibit high negative emotions. They are irritable and tend to be emotionally upset. They are prone to direct their anger and verbal aggression to others. Their tendency to cry is associated with fear.

Antagonism: Similarly, to children who express high levels of negative emotions, the antagonist is aggressive and exhibits antisocial behaviour such as rudeness. They break the rules and tend to be disrespectful to adults.

Strong-Willed: Children are perceived to be stubborn and argumentative and have a strong tendency to want to impose their will on others. They want their way and always seek to be dominant in social interactions.

Distractibility: Children who obtain a high score on this scale have a low ability to self-regulate attention toward getting long-range goals. They generally have a short attention span and are more forgetful than their peers.

Disorganized: Disorganized children are careless and tend to be messy. Their need for order is very low.

Inhibition-to-the-Unfamiliar: Children high in inhibition avoid people and new situations. When it is impossible to avoid new situations, they look for a way out or sit passively observing the people and the surrounding. Martin et al. (2020), however, points out that "they may warm up to the new situation, given time, and become progressively less apprehensive. However, they take longer to integrate into new social situations than their peers" (15).

Insecure/Fearful: Children with such characteristics are insecure about their abilities and social acceptance. They are generally fearful.

Social Withdrawal: These children prefer to be by themselves and "prefer the world of things" rather than "the world of people". They are socially isolated.

Compliance: The compliant child adapts quickly to the rules and expectations of adults. They have a desire to please others.

Table 1.1: Higher-Order Behavioural Tendencies

Higher-order behavioral tendency	Scales measuring these constructs
Academic Ability	Intelligence
	Openness-To-Experience
Achievement Motivation	Achievement Motivation
Prosocial Behavior	Positive Emotionality
	Consideration-of-Others
Activity Level	Activity Level
Irritability/Antagonism	Negative Emotionality
	Antagonism
	Strong-Willed Behavior
Poor Attention Regulation	Distractibility
	Disorganization
Social Withdrawal/Shy	Social Withdrawal
	Inhibition to the Unfamiliar
Insecure/Fearful	Insecurity/Fearfulness

Source: (Martin, Lease and Slobodskaya 2020, 18)

As the researchers examined these fifteen characteristics, they recognized that some of the characteristics correlated with one another. The researchers then regrouped the fifteen characteristics into six broader behaviour tendencies: positive emotionality, prosocial behaviour, negative emotionality/irritability, distractibility (ability to control attentions), activity level and inhibition of the unfamiliar (shyness) (see table 1.1).

These individual differences in children can exert influence on the child's life throughout their life span. This is because of the relative degree of stability of temperament throughout an individual's life span. The degree of stability in temperament is largely influenced by genetic mechanism and a stable environment.

Genetic Mechanism and Temperaments

There are two approaches to study genetics: behaviour genetics or quantitative genetics. Scientists in a quest to understand temperamental differences study relatives, for example, monozygotic and dizygotic twins, cousins and siblings. In this study, no DNA is collected. Instead, "comparisons are made of the similarities in behaviour across varying degree of biological relatedness" (Martin, Lease and Slobodskaya 2020, 160).

Identical twins share 100 per cent of their genes (DNA) and are more similar in their behaviour than fraternal twins, who share 50 per cent of their DNA on average; both categories of twins show similarity in their behaviours than individuals who are not related. Twins are critical in the quest to understand behavioural styles among children; they allow for studying the environmental influences and varying genetic makeup. The heritability of behaviour is used to measure the extent to which a behaviour is inherited on a continuum of 0 to 1. Heritability can be defined as a proportion of the variability observed in a sample of children that differences in genetic similarity can explain. "Heritability is an estimate of the genotype of the individual" (Martin et al. 2020, 160). Martin et al. pointed out that "A behavior determined to be highly heritable, like academic intelligence, has a heritability score in the 0.60–0.80 range" (160). Whereas "measured behavioral pattern (anxiety, leadership, or irritability) is referred to as the phenotype and is composed of genetically related factors as well as environmental factors. Using these techniques, the heritability of most temperamental and later developing personality characteristics is moderate (0.30–0.60)" (160).

There are two types of environmental effects that are also estimates for behavioural genetics: non-shared environment and shared environment. When siblings and twins are raised in the same family, we have the shared environment effects; when twins and siblings are raised in different families the non-shared environment concerns, "the non-shared environment is associated with differences in parental treatment of children in the family, sibling interactions, effects of accident or illness on individual children, and influences outside the home such as peers. A behavioural trait might have a heritability of 0.50, a shared environment effect of 0.20, and a non-shared environmental influence of 0.30" (Martin et al. 2020, 160). Bratko, Butkovie and Hlupie (2017) concluded the following from their metananlysis about temperament and genetics using all available behavioural genetic studies published before 2010:

- intraclass correlations for monozygotic twin pairs (reared together as well as those reared apart) are larger than intraclass correlations for dizygotic twin pairs. This indicates that there is a genetic effect underlying individual differences in personality
- intraclass correlations of twin pairs raised together are very similar to those of pairs raised apart, indicated that sharing family environment does not contribute to their similarity
- intraclass correlations for monozygotic twin pairs (reared together as well as those reared apart) are more than twice the intraclass correlations for dizygotic twin pairs (12).

In addition, scientists have been conducting molecular genetic studies to identify specific genes that contribute to various behaviour traits. For example, there are certain genes such as serotonergic genes which "have been implicated in mood disorders, alcoholism and certain personality traits" (Ham et al. 2004, 2).

Interactions between Temperament and the Environment: Theoretical Frameworks

The environments experienced by most children varied. Both the school and home environment make different demands on a child. McClowry (2014) identified Goodness of Fit and The Diathesis-Stress Model as the theories used to explain the association between children's temperaments and their environment. Both the school and home environment make different demands on a child. How these environments, with their demands and expectations, exert influence on children's actions and reactions depend on the child's temperament.

Goodness of Fit

Goodness of fit refers to the extent that the child's temperament matches the features of the environment. The characteristics of the environment include the values, expectations, demands and the characteristics or temperaments of the adults (Keogh 2003; McClowry 2014). A child's temperament may fit with a parent's temperament and expectation or may be intrusive and disruptive. Similarly, the child's temperament may not fit with the expectations and demands of the teacher in the classroom.

Chess (1990) explained that in addition to identifying from each of the New York longitudinal participants' temperaments, parents and teachers provided insights into their expectations and demands on each child. In each case, Chess reported that there was excessive conflict in the interaction between the child's temperamental qualities and the environmental demands and expectations. On the other hand, Chess noted that where parental and social demands were consistent with the child's temperament, "there were few cases of maladjustment" (121). Hence, "goodness of fit" environment resulted. A goodness of fit happens "when environmental expectations and demands of parents and others were consonant with the child's temperamental characteristics" (321). On the other hand, poorness of fit occurs when there is a conflict between a child's temperament and the demands and expectations of others (parents, teachers and so on). A child's optimal development is possible in a goodness of fit environment (Chess 1990). However, a poorness of fit environment can thwart a child's development. Keogh (2003) explains how a child's temperament can be associated with goodness of fit environment:

> slow-to-warm-up children may not do well in fast-paced instructional programs and maybe be overwhelmed in free-flowing "open" classrooms where there is a high level of activity and where routines change daily, even hourly. Intense, active, and impulsive children may have problems in classes with rigidly defined rules and work periods that demand persistence and quiet concentration over long periods. It is important to note that teachers, too, differ in temperament – some being highly active, intense and impulsive, others being slow in tempo, slow-to-warm-up, and shy. Fast-paced teachers may see shy and withdrawing children as unresponsive and unmotivated, while more reticent, slow-to-warm-up teachers may see the behavior of high energy and intense children as troublesome. (3)

As temperament develops, a new system of behavioural organization can come into action over time. According to Rothbart and Bates (2006), "any new systems that serve to regulate action and emotion will also come to modulate characteristics that were previously present yielding potential instability of temperament across the developmental transition" (127). In other words, children can learn to manage the negative reactive side of their personality over time by developing a control system. So, as Rothbart and Bates pointed out, the child who develops certain controls (for example, self-regulation competencies) early in life may have different experiences from those who develop such control system later in their development. Any failure of proper controls can lead to behavioural problems.

The Diathesis-Stress Model

In the Diathesis-Stress Model temperamental predispositions are individual differences, thought by most researchers to be the result of genetic differences in the "'biochemical soup' that regulates neurological activity. Thus, variation in observed or measured temperament is thought to result from (a) variation in levels of brain peptides, neurotransmitters, hormones and enzymes as they affect primarily limbic structure of the brain and from (b) environmental events that affect and are affected by these physiological differences" (Martin 1994, 122).

The Diathesis-Stress Model advocate that there is an interaction between various types of environments and an individual's predisposition risk. They are challenges of an individual's temperament "that places the individual at high or low risk for developing behavioural problems" (McClowry 2014). According to McClowry, students that have easy temperament "are generally at low risk for developing behaviour problems" (15). Whereas children who have challenging temperament, the high dispositional risk under certain stressful situation, are likely to develop more serious behavioural problems. Figure 1.1 illustrates the central thesis of the Diathesis-Stress Model. The horizontal line presents possible home and school environments, while the vertical axis is the predispositional risk that is attributed to a child's temperament.

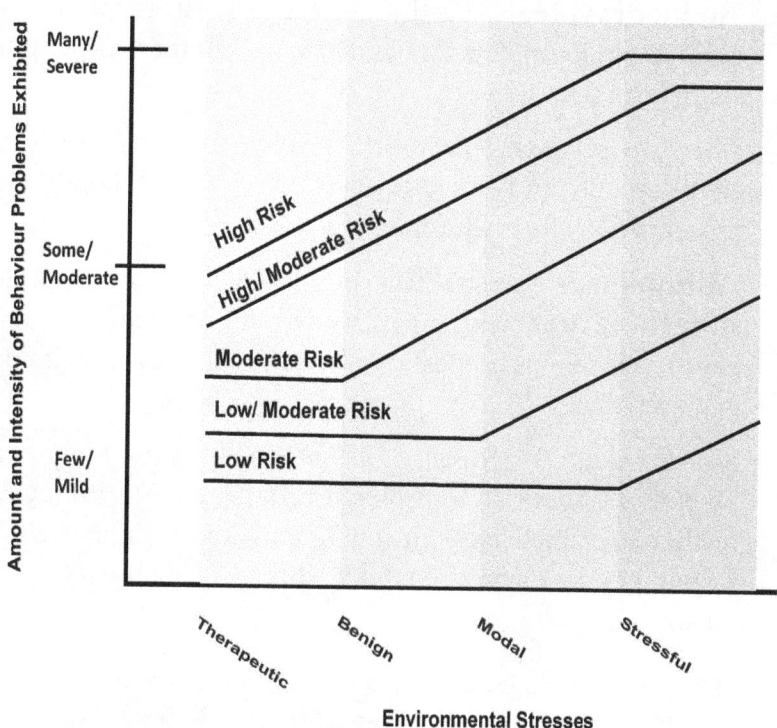

Figure 1.1: Hypothetical Relation between Environmental Stress and Behaviour Problems as Mediated by Predispositional Risk

There are various levels of stress in different environments. The Diathesis, for simplification, proposes five levels of environmental stressfulness. The levels are as follows:

Therapeutic: at this level, the environment is very accepting of individuals and accept individual differences in behaviours and learning. The environment provides support for learning and growth.

Benign: This environment is not therapeutic but does foster stresses necessary to produce behavioural problems.

Modal or typical: This third level is likely to be the general experiences in schools and homes in which there is periodic short-term stress.

Chronic stress: This fourth level is stressful. Such an environment can involve the poverty level of a family, the presence of a clinically depressed parent, etc.

Pathological Stress: This fifth level is a pathologically stressful environment. In this environment, there is child abuse, continuous domestic violence or families in the midst of a war zone.

Environmental Stress influences individuals at predispositional risk to problem behaviours. Martin (1994) further explained how an individual's temperament could respond to the environmental factors by using the following illustration:

> A highly active child has a good fit with the environment of the sports playing field but has a bad fit with the demands for quiet, cognitive performance typical of the elementary classroom. The child who has difficulty adapting to changing environments may have trouble adjusting to the middle or junior high school, since in this context there is much shifting from classroom to classroom, with different social groups and classroom rules. (126)

Both theories, the Goodness of Fit Model and the Diathesis-Stress Model, agree that behaviour styles, that is, temperaments, interact with environmental factors. Such interaction may play a critical role in the development of children's healthy or delinquent behaviours.

Summary

In this chapter, we defined temperament as the consistent behavioural styles of individuals. A discussion followed this as to why educators, parents and other caregivers should gain some understanding of temperament. Temperament influences social interactions and hence the interaction between children and adults. Teachers and parents in understanding children's temperament can predict patterns of behaviour and plan the appropriate environment.

Kagan and Snidman (2004) conducted longitudinal research tracking an individual's temperament from infancy to adolescence. The researchers found that, for example, low reactive children were more likely to report that they were happy most of the time. Kagan and Snidman also found that the environment in which children grew up can modify their temperament.

The two theories, Goodness of Fit and the Diathesis-Stress models, discussed how important the environment is in influencing the expression of temperament. The environment can exacerbate the negative reactivity of temperament or enhance the positive dimension of an individual's temperament. Goodness of Fit occurs when the environment accommodates temperaments. So, for example, children who are shy and cautious would benefit more from teachers' extensive time and attention than children who are task persistent. The Diathesis-Stress Model advocates that a person with a certain temperament or disposition can be more vulnerable to stress than other temperaments. According to the Diathesis-Stress, individuals who have a disposition to depression, given a stressful environment, are likely to become depressed. This happens because of their dispositional risk that is exacerbated by the environmental situation.

2. Understanding Parents' Interactions with Their Children

It is within the microsystem – the home – where parents are the main actors. It is within the home that infants and children are taught socially acceptable behaviours and develop self-regulating skills that allow for healthy social interactions. Likewise, deviant, antisocial behaviours can result from the home environment, which can ultimately lead to problem behaviours in young children. The quality of the parent-child relationship, mother-and-father relationship, and the parent interaction and practices does influence the development of delinquent behaviours, such as aggressive behaviour in children. Socialization in the home does not eliminate deviant behaviours, but it "moderates its expression and changes its form" (Hamby and Grych 2013, 51).

Parenting has a critical impact on a child's development at the preschool and elementary levels because of the immediate and direct effects of parental discipline practices and nurturance (Marcus 2017). Ineffective parenting, such as the lack of parental warmth and over-permissiveness in the development of children through to adolescence can result in children feeling disconnected, rejected and aggressive (Calvete et al. 2015). The parent-child relationship formed early in a child's development sets the stage for long-term future ties with members of the wider society. Also, this early bond or attachment between parent and child influences social interaction competences, quality of friendships and aggressive behaviours later in the individual's life (Marcus 2017).

Parent-child Relationship Attachment

The quality of the parent-child relationship is determined by the early emotional bond between the two persons. The psychological concept of *attachment* is used by researchers to examine and understand the quality of the emotional bond between children and parents. Attachment is a strong emotional bond with special persons in our lives that leads us to feel pleasure and security when we interact with them. These persons provide comfort by proximity to them in times of stress (Berk 2014). Attachment behaviour increases the feelings of closeness and belonging of the child to the attachment figure, who is usually the mother (Cassidy 1999; Hong and Park 2012). A child's interest in an attachment, that is, interacting with the mother is expressed via attachment behaviours, such as smiling or vocalizing (Cassidy). These behaviours signal the interest of the child to the mother; other behaviours, such as crying, bring the mother to the child to terminate discomfort and distress. This "affectional bond" is continual, not transient. This bond involves a specific person who cannot be easily replaced by others. The relationship in this bond is emotionally significant, the individual experiences a feeling of distress at involuntary separation from the attachment figure. The relationship is one of security and comfort for the individual. The attachment is said to be "secure" if security is achieved and "insecure" if it is not achieved. It is the seeking for security that is the core principle of the attachment theory.

In examining infants' relationships with their parents, Ainsworth-Salter et al. (1978) identified four patterns of bonding between infants and their caregivers (usually the mothers). These patterns were investigated in a laboratory setting, and the quality of attachment at one and two years of age was assessed in what they termed "strange situations". These strange situations were presented in eight episodes in which there were brief separations and reunions with mothers (see table 2.1).

Table 2.1:   Summary of Episodes of the Strange Situation

Number of Episode	Persons Present	Duration	Brief Description of Action
1	Mother, baby, & observer	30 secs.	Observer introduces mother and baby to experimental room, then leaves.
2	Mother & baby	3 min.	Mother is nonparticipant while baby explores; if necessary, play is stimulated after 2 minutes.
3	Stranger, mother, & baby	3 min.	Stranger enters. First minute: Stranger silent. Second minute: Stranger converses with mother. Third minute: Stranger approaches baby. After 3 minutes mother leaves unobtrusively.
4	Stranger & baby	3 min. or less[a]	First separation episode. Stranger's behavior is geared to that of baby.
5	Mother & baby	3 min. or more[b]	First reunion episode. Mother greets and/or comforts baby, then tries to settle him again in play. Mother then leaves, saying "bye-bye."
6	Baby alone	3 min. or less[a]	Second separation episode.
7	Stranger & baby	3 min. or less[a]	Continuation of second separation. Stranger enters and gears her behavior to that of baby.
8	Mother & baby	3 min.	Second reunion episode. Mother enters, greets baby, then picks him up. Meanwhile stranger leaves unobtrusively.

[a]Episode is curtailed if the baby is unduly distressed.
[b]Episode is prolonged if more time is required for the baby to become re-involved in play.

The following were identified as attachment patterns:

Secure attachment: The secure group of infants (one to two years old) enjoyed harmonious interactions with their mothers. When separated from their mothers, they would cry, but only for a very short period. In other words, they expressed very little distress and showed positive greetings upon reunion. These secure babies tend to be compliant to their mother's wishes and to be less angry. The mothers of infants who experienced secure attachments had long bouts of interactions with their infants. Mothers of the secure infants initiated more interactions than mothers of the other groups and were more positive in their behaviour towards their infants. These mothers did more stimulating activities with their children by engaging in exploratory play that reflected their children's interests. The mothers also exhibited positive feelings and emotions towards their children. These mothers were more sensitive in communicating with their children and less angry and rejecting (Ainsworth et al. 1978).

Avoidant attachment: Avoidant attachment infants were unresponsive to their mothers when they were present; when the mothers left, they were usually not distressed. These children seemed to recognize their mothers but were indifferent during the reunion. When they were picked up, they failed to cling (Ainsworth et al. 1987; Berk 2014). Mothers of avoidant infants were less affectionate when holding the baby. These mothers withheld important feedback from their babies during their interaction with them. They were also less aware of their infants' signals for interactions and less responsive to them (Ainsworth et al. 1978).

Resistant attachment: Before separation, resistant attachment infants sought closeness to their mothers and, for most of the time, they failed to explore. They manifest intense anger. Their resistance is shown by "pushing away from, striking out at, or squirming to get down from an adult who has offered contact, or by pushing away, throwing away, or otherwise rejecting toys through which an adult attempt to mediate interaction" (Ainsworth et al. 1978, 53). The infants in this group were extremely angry and distressed during separation. When their mothers return, they combine anger with clinginess and resistive behaviour, sometimes hitting and pushing (Berk 2014). The caregivers for these infants are usually less prompt and consistent in responding to the infants' signal for interactions (Ainsworth et al. 1978).

Disoriented/disorganized: This group was added by Main and Solomon (1986). This is the group of infants with the greatest insecurity. They look away from the mother while being held by the mother, and they approach the mother with "flat, depressed emotion" (Berk 2014, 198). They also exhibit a dazed facial expression (Berk 2014). The mothers of this group are helpless emotionally and are hostile and confrontational. The researchers describe them as "abdicating the protection function of the caregiving system … they are conflict-laden, disengaged and hostile" (Solomon and George 2011, 5).

Research shows that avoidant attachment infants, because of their insecurity experience, tend to have a constant sense of rejection as they mature. This group of children seems not to express anger directly in close relationships but tend to withdraw and become emotionally disconnected (Moretti and Peled 2004). The child with disoriented attachment in infancy has a strong propensity to be involved with aggressive behaviour. Bowlby (1988) noted that both parents are needed as a secure base for the infants as they develop to journey into the outside world. Children with disorganized attachment, that is, children who have been traumatized by their parents' behaviour from early in their development exhibit aggressive behaviour (Delker, Bernstein and Laurent 2018; Goodman, Bartlett and Stroh 2013; and Lyons-Ruth 1996). Delker et al. (2018) expanded by noting that poverty does affect the quality of attachment and children's risky behaviours, which includes aggression: "If raised in poverty or near poverty, adolescents with disorganised attachment histories reported significantly more risk-taking behaviors than adolescents with secure attachment histories. The long-term association between these early developmental contexts and later risk-taking is particularly noteworthy when considering that the focal moderation finding was observed above and beyond the effect of concurrent family economic hardship in the child's adolescence" (292).

Parents reduce the risk of children experiencing harm when they love and care for their infants from an early stage. High-quality love communication between parents and children will result in the children becoming confident and self-reliant as they mature when exploring the world. On the other hand, when a child's attachment behaviours are responded to by both parents in a tardy and unwilling manner, the child develops anxiety and a strong sense of rejection. Planalp and Braungart-Ricker's (2013) findings support the above. Their study revealed that both parents, mother and father, were less responsive and sensitive to the emotional needs of avoidant infants. The researchers observed that avoidant infants displayed fewer attachment behaviours in comparison to secure or disorganized infants.

Of the four patterns of infant attachment, the disoriented/disorganized attachment is the pattern that is highly correlated with aggressive behaviours (Lyons-Ruth 1996). According to Lyons-Ruth, aggressive behaviours by children are usually a reflection of poor relationships with parents. Disoriented/disorganized attachment infants tend to experience apprehension, helplessness and prolonged freezing. This attachment pattern is associated with mothers who have a high consumption rate of alcohol, mothers who are depressed, as well as adolescent mothers (Carlson 1998; Lyons-Ruth 1996). Disorganized attachment results from the "lack of, or collapse of a consistent strategy for organizing responses to the need for comfort and security when under stress" (Lyons-Ruth 1996, 67). Carlson concluded from her longitudinal study involving children, aged twenty-four months to nineteen years, that infants who exhibited disorganized attachment behaviours were highly associated with environmental factors, such as the quality of the caregiving relationship (whether the caregiver was sensitive or insensitive) and the socio-economic condition of the mothers living alone with the infants. Carlson's study also revealed that disorganized infants, as they develop, can cause behavioural problems in pre-elementary and elementary schools. Several researchers' findings revealed that infants who show disorganized attachment behaviour towards their mothers later became aggressive (Greenberg et al. 1993; Pasco Fearon and Belsky 2011; O'Connor et al. 2014). From their findings, Pasco Fearon and Belsky concluded: "The current results provide further evidence that individual differences in attachment behavior are associated with differences in children's behavior problems in the school years. They further indicate that the effects of attachment disorganization may increase over time" (790).

Parents' stress also impacts on children (Tharner et al. 2012; Beernink et al. 2012). Tharner et al. found that infant attachment patterns influenced the effect of parenting stress on three-year-old children's emotional and behaviour problems. The higher the parenting stress, the more likely it was for children with an insecure attachment pattern in infancy to display withdrawal or aggressive behaviour. The avoidant children exhibit more internalizing behaviour, while the disorganized types displayed more externalizing behaviours. The three-year-old children who experienced secure attachment were able to buffer the influence of parenting stress.

The attachment process between infant and caregiver is foundational in the infant's development as a secure individual. The attachment provides the earliest means by which children learn self-regulatory skills (Reebye 2005). However, as evidenced in table 3, it was always the mothers who were involved in Ainsworth-Salter et al.'s (1978) Strange Situations study. Similar to Ainsworth et al. (1978), Bowlby (1988) felt that the mother is the primary caregiver for the child and therefore exerts more influence over the infant than the father.

It is important not to minimize the father's contribution to attachment and not to generalize the mother's attachment to the infant to be the same as the father's. Developmental texts such as Berk's (2014) generalize Ainsworth's et al. findings to both parents; in so doing, students of developmental psychology may not distinguish the different impact that both parents have on a child's development. There is a growing body of literature (Lamb 1977; Lamb 2010; McKenzie and Casselman 2017; Delker, Bernstein and Laurent 2018), which speaks to the role of the father in a child's development. In 1977, Lamb reported qualitative differences in the interaction between infant and father, and infant and mother. Lamb noted that in his observation at six months following the time when attachment relations are to emerge, there was no difference in the infant attachment to both parents. Lamb found that children looked to both mother and father for comfort whenever the need arose. Also, Lamb's study shows that the mother-infant and father-infant relationship provides different kinds of experiences for the infants. For example, Lamb found that mothers often hold the child, and provide physical contact to perform caretaking functions, while fathers hold the child and provide physical contact through play with the child. While the older infants were held less for caretaking functions, the older infants were held more for play. Lamb concluded that the nature of mother-infant and father-infant interactions differ qualitatively but were required consistently in the child's life. Lamb concluded that "the fact that mothers and fathers consistently engage their infants in different types of interaction suggests that infants may be able to distinguish the two parents on behavioural as well as perceptual criteria" (168). This also suggests that both parents are likely to have a different impact on children's behaviour. The literature indicates that the rejection of fathers, similar to that of mothers, results in children experiencing negative emotions, such as sadness, anger, and resentment; these children are more likely to develop aggressive tendencies.

Attachment and Temperament

The empirical evidence showing a relationship between temperament and attachment is scanty. Though the research is not conclusive, there are studies (Goldsmith and Harman 1994; Kornienko 2016; van den Boom 1994; Stams, Juffer and van IJzendoorn 2002) that suggest some interaction between temperament and attachment. Attachment and temperament share a common ground in that they both refer to emotional individuality (Goldsmith and Harman 1994). Attachment, as we discussed earlier, refer primarily to the emotional bond between caregiver and infant. Temperament includes "activity level, fearfulness, irritability, joyfulness, and a variety of other behavioural tendencies" (Goldsmith and Harman 1994, 53). Attachment and temperament have the following features: they are primarily emotional in nature, appear in infancy, are fairly stable over a period of time and are biologically based (Goldsmith and Harman 1994; Berk 2010). Attachment quality refers primarily to one of the security aspects of the infant-mother relationship (Goldsmith and Harman 1994). Security involves trust and love.

Despite the lack of conclusive findings about the association between a child's temperament and the quality of attachment between mother and child, Goldsmith and Harman (1994) speculated a possibility that attachment and temperament have a reciprocal influence on each other. In 1994, van den Boom's reported improved attachment quality when mothers with infants who were irritable in their temperament received an intervention. Van den Boom's results suggested that children's temperament could affect the quality of attachment. However, with intervention, mothers could change their approach and thus improve the quality of the attachment. Stams, Juffer and van IJzendoorn (2002) conducted a longitudinal study examining 146 internationally adopted children who were placed before six months of age. These children were followed by researchers from infancy to seven years of age. The study revealed children with difficult temperament (high in distractibility and low in task persistence) presented challenges to the quality of an attachment between mother and child. Stams, Juffer and van IJzendoorn (2002) noted:

> In biological families, genetic relatedness may dampen the effects of children's temperament, because shared genes might make it easier to stimulate the goodness of fit between parent and offspring. The current study emphasizes the importance of difficult temperament for later adjustment in families where temperamental commonalities between parents and children are contingent instead of genetically based. It should be noted that the least favourable type of attachment, that is, attachment disorganization, did not uniquely predict (mal) adaptation in middle childhood. In the current investigation, attachment disorganization only predicted later adjustment in interaction with difficult temerament. (815–16)

In 2016, Kornienko examined the role of child temperament in maternal relationship with their child. Temperament in this study is defined as "as inherent individual differences in self-regulation or in attentional, emotional, and motor reactivity [1] and, according to Thomas and Chess [1977] expresses itself in behavioural responses across contexts" (342). The results showed an association between a child's temperament and their relationship with their mother. Kornienko noted:

> That child's temperament plays an important role in the parent's relationship with a child. Child temperament traits predict a mother's relation in less than 10% of cases. Adaptability and Quality of mood are predictors for all mother's relations to child characteristics, except control. At the same time, distractible boys cause more controlling reactions in mothers. These facts support the findings that difficult temperament makes parents more consistent, colder, and less satisfied with their relation to their child. It also supports the idea of Belsky's process model about the impact of child temperament on its relationship with parents. (346)

Belsky's process model suggests that a child's temperament may play a role in influencing parents' behaviour. Belsky's cited a study by Campbell (1979) that found, "when mothers rated their infants as having difficult temperaments at three months, they interacted with them less and were less responsive to their cries at three and eight months" (86). Hence an infant's temperament can play a role in the quality of attachment between mother and child.

Child-rearing Styles

According to Berk (2014), child-rearing styles include "parenting behaviours that occur over a wide range of situations, creating an enduring child-rearing climate" (278). Parents' discipline practices permeate the child-rearing climate of any home. Tremblay et al. (2008) noted that discipline is more than punishing a child, "it is teaching children to stop, wait, speak, and solve problems" (19); such practices can create a warm and nurturing climate in which children develop as wholesome adults. Baumrind (1971) generated three categories of child-rearing styles, based on observing parents' interaction with their preschoolers: authoritative, authoritarian and permissive. In the 1980s, *neglect* was added as a child-rearing style (Berk 2014). The popular categories of child-rearing styles (Baumrind 1971) are as follows:

- Authoritative: This involves a combination of high control and positive encouragement. Even though parents are controlling and demanding, "they are warm, rational, and receptive to the child's communication" (1). Authoritative parents encourage verbal give-and-take and listen to the child's reasoning concerning issues. Such parents affirm the child's characteristics, differences, and unique attributes, and always challenge the child by setting standards for conduct. According to Baumrind (1971), the authoritative parent "uses reason as well as the power to achieve her objectives" (22). Chao (2001) is of the view that the authoritative parenting style is the most effective because it fosters close and mutually satisfying relationships with the children.

- Authoritarian: Authoritarian parents are controlling and detached. They are not warm towards their children. These parents value obedience and set unnegotiable standards of discipline. They favour punitive and forceful measures to control self-will. According to Baumrind (1971), these parents believe in "inculcating such instrumental values as respect for authority, respect for work and respect for the preservation of order and traditional structure" (22).
- Permissive/indulgent: Permissive parents are not controlling, not demanding and are relatively warm and affectionate. Permissive parents have an accepting and affirming disposition towards their children. They tend to consult with the children concerning rules and policy decisions. Children are not required to do household duties, and there is no communication by the parents regarding standards of expected behaviour. Children are allowed to regulate their behaviour; there is no system of accountability (Baumrind 1971).
- Neglectful/uninvolved: Parents with the neglectful/uninvolved child-rearing style have low acceptance of their parental role and minimal involvement in their child's development. These parents are somewhat indifferent and detached emotionally from their child. They are also bewildered by life stresses, lethargic and uninvolved in the activities of their child. Children of uninvolved parents experience neglect, which is a form of maltreatment (Berk 2014).

Parental demands can incite behavioural problems, such as aggression in children. The literature, however, is inconclusive about the ideal parenting style. Authoritarian and permissive parenting styles were reported to produce negative dispositions in children, while the authoritative parenting style has been touted as the ideal parenting style (Baumrind 1971, 1991; Hart, Newell and Olson 2008; Grusec, Davidov and Lundell 2002). Baumrind's findings (1971) revealed that through the developmental stages of a child's life, authoritative parents seemed to protect their adolescents from drug problems and negative behaviours. Baumrind (1991) highlighted that authoritative parent provides the necessary control that young adult experience developmentally. Children from authoritative upbringing had more self-regulatory skills, discouraging problem behaviours in boys and girls at all developmental stages (Baumrind 1991). Parents who are authoritative in their parenting style were adaptable to their children's disposition, and they were gentle and engaged in reasoning-oriented regulations (Hart, Newell and Olson 2008). Hart, Newell and Olsen (2008) concluded that of the other parenting patterns, authoritative parents' flexibility provides a goodness of fit environment for children with varying temperamental profiles. Despite the above discussion on the advantages of the authoritative parenting style, Garcia and Garcia's (2009) findings revealed that adolescents who characterized their parents as authoritative and permissive were associated with more positive outcomes than adolescents with authoritarian and neglectful parents. However, overall, the researchers' findings revealed that adolescents whose parents used the permissive child-rearing style scored equal or better and yielded positive scores on self-esteem, psychological adjustment, personal competence and problem behaviour outcomes. The researchers, therefore, concluded that, for Spain, the optimum style of parenting is the permissive one.

Concerning the neglect, child-rearing style studies (Demeusy et al 2018; Knutson, Degarmo and Koeppl 2005; Kotch et al. 2008) confirm that a child who experiences neglect from early in his or her development (younger than two years old) is likely to develop increased behavioural problems, such as childhood aggression. Kotch et al., following a longitudinal study, concluded that "child neglect in the first two years of life may be a more-important precursor of childhood aggression than later neglect or physical abuse at any age" (725). Demeusy's et al.'s results also confirm that parental neglect is a strong predictor of childhood aggression. They noted, based on their investigation, that a significant predictor of high levels of aggression in children was neglect by parents.

In addition to child-rearing styles exhibited by parents, parents have the responsibility to create a nurturing environment that will facilitate their children's development. The interaction between children's unique temperaments and their environment influences their behaviour (Chess 1990; Churchill 2003; Smiley et al. 2016; Hipson and Seguin 2016). Chess advocates the importance for adults to understand children's temperaments and create a goodness-of-fit environment. Such an environment is conducive to children's characteristics, which will ultimately enhance their social and emotional development. An important task of parents, especially during the early years of children's development, is to manage their children's behaviour. This involves creating an environment that enhances the children's positives and equips the young ones with social and coping skills that will help them to manage the negative reactivity of their temperament (McClowry and Graham 2014). Because parents are adults, they have the primary responsibility to adjust their behaviour to help the children learn appropriate behaviour and coping strategies. Smiley et al.'s (2016) findings support the goodness-of-fit model. They found that a "mother's negativity during teaching is a poor fit for children who are low in interest and a mother's warmth during task-focused interactions buffers against helplessness when children are high in sadness" (299). Intervening early in behaviour issues among preschoolers, with involvement from parents, could enhance parental practices and result in improved child behaviour. Laukkanen et al. (2014) based on their results suggest that it is prudent to advise mothers that the use of psychological control may increase rather than decrease a child's distress and negative emotion in daily life. According to Laukkanen et al., by telling mothers that their child low positivity and high activity is as a result of the child's temperament rather than bad behaviour may help the mother's well-being and tendency to practice adaptive parenting. Laukkanen et al. examined the association between children's temperament and mothers' parenting styles. Laukkanen et al. reported that "...the more active and the less positive a mother perceived her child to be, the lower was her well-being and, consequently, the more psychological control she applied". Low positivity temperament was high in negative reaction; they were fussy and cried frequently.

Summary

This chapter emphasized parents' interactions with their children and how such interactions can affect the quality of the home environment in which children developed. We looked at different forms of attachment and child-rearing styles and how these various forms shape the parent-child relationship.

Attachment, which is the emotional bond between parent and child, is discussed. In examining attachment, Ainsworth et al. identified four patterns of bonding: secure attachment, avoidant attachment, resistant attachment and disoriented or disorganized attachment. We explored the connection between attachment and temperament. Though the literature is not conclusive, some studies show an association between attachment and temperament. Investigations revealed that infants with irritable temperament tend to lower the positive quality of attachment between mother and child.

Parents interact with their children through the strategies they use for behavioural management of their children.

These strategies are called child-rearing styles. We discussed four popular categories of child-rearing style: authoritative, authoritarian, permissive/indulgent and neglectful/uninvolved. It is these child-rearing styles that create the environment necessary for the healthy development of the child. A goodness of fit environment is conducive to the children's characteristics, which ultimately affect the child's social and emotional development.

Parents sometimes need help in creating goodness of fit environment for the child. Early intervention can help a parent to see the child's negative reactions as temperament rather than bad behaviour. This will help the parent to understand his or her responsibility in helping the child develop proper controls early in their development.

3. School Factors and Temperament

During the early years, teachers are likely to play the role of the parent-surrogate in the classroom, thereby developing relationships with children that significantly impact their development. This chapter discusses the school factors such as teacher-student relationships and peers. We discussed the teacher-child relationships and how children's different temperaments impact the relationship. The reciprocal nature of the interactions between teachers and students can aggravate students' disruptive behaviour. The influence of family relations on peer relationships is examined and how family impacts peer relationships at school.

The early childhood teacher not only disciplines and rewards a child, but wipes the tears and running noses, comforts hurt feelings and mediates in peer conflicts. Similar to the parent-child relationship, the teacher-child relationship varies in nature and quality (Howes, Hamilton and Matheson 1994; Runions et al. 2014; Yoleri 2016). Howes et al. (1994) found a negative correlation between the toddler's security with the teacher and behavioural problems. When toddlers' security with the teacher was high, their problem behaviour was low, and vice versa. Also, Howes et al. found that pre-schoolers who were shy and withdrawn were too dependent on the teacher.

Runions et al.'s (2014) results from their longitudinal study (pre-kindergarten to grade one) revealed that teacher-child conflicts in kindergarten predicted children's engagement in aggressive behaviour in grade 1. As this was a quantitative study, the reason for this occurrence was not forthcoming.

Teacher-student conflict can be buttressed when teacher-student relationships experience repetitive, negative patterns that McClowry (1999) calls "getting stuck". This situation of getting stuck with disruptive students tends to escalate with students experiencing ongoing increases in negative behaviour and the teacher being frustrated (Thomas et al. 2011; Nelson and Roberts 2000). Nelson and Roberts (2000) found that teachers reacted negatively to disruptive students. There were recurring negative relationships between students and teachers. Nelson and Roberts's findings highlighted the following:

- Teachers tend to interact negatively with children with behavioural disorders.
- For some students, disruptive behaviour was an event (occurring only once) while, for others, disruptive behaviour was a chain, involving several reciprocal exchanges.
- To children with disruptive and aggressive behaviours, teachers gave more commands and reprimands in comparison to non-disruptive or non-aggressive students.

The general negative approach of teachers must be viewed within an ongoing reciprocal context. Children who exhibit disruptive behaviours typically engage in behaviours that are offensive to those with whom they interact. The continuing reciprocal nature of the interactions may cause teachers to respond more negatively towards students who exhibit disruptive behaviours than to those who do not.

Children's problem behaviours can be aggravated by teacher-student relationships characterized by conflict (Meehan, Hughes and Cavell 2003; Doumen et al. 2008; Gallagher

2014). Meehan et al., following a two-year investigation of an association between the quality of teacher-student relationship and disruptive behaviour at the primary level, concluded that students' levels of problem behaviours such as aggression were related to the quality of teacher-child relationship (indicators of quality were intimacy, affection, admiration, satisfaction and reliable alliance). Doumen et al.'s findings revealed that children's disruptive behaviour and conflict with their teacher increased from the beginning of the academic year in kindergarten to the end of the academic year. The researchers speculated that this conflict in teacher-student relationships could reflect a teacher's general negative attitude towards a child. High levels of teacher-student conflicts at the beginning of kindergarten can predict increased levels of problem behaviour at the end of the academic year in kindergarten (Gallagher 2014).

Frustrated teachers, similar to frustrated parents, may rely on ineffective and negative behavioural strategies, such as commands, threats and other counterproductive measures to increase compliance from children. Such negative controls by teachers may merely reinforce children's oppositional behaviours. Teacher-student relationships, characterized by a teacher's disapproval, undermine effective learning and strengthen disruptive behaviour (Thomas et al. 2008; Webster-Stratton and Herman 2010). Webster-Stratton and Herman (2010), noted that "if elementary school teachers of such children fail to consistently provide responsive and nurturing teaching, reinforcement for prosocial behavior, and effective proactive discipline, a coercive cycle may be established whereby children's oppositional and negative behaviour is reinforced by the teachers' harsh or critical responses or giving in to their demands" (38). Teacher-student conflicts aggravate students' problem behaviours. Teachers, as the adults in the relationship, have the responsibility to create an environment conducive to learning and geared toward minimizing personal conflict with the children who are minors in the relation. Teachers have a fiduciary duty to students in the classroom, as they are entrusted with children by parents and society to act with care and professionalism.

The teachers' relationships with their students are essential to create and support social-emotional stability among students in the classroom environment. High levels of negativity in teacher-child relationships seem to predict children's adjustment to school, especially at the elementary level. The predominant attributes of teacher-student relationships seem to depend on the levels of warmth, trust, closeness and conflict. Therefore, high-quality teacher-student relationships involve high levels of warmth, closeness and low levels of conflict. Students' socio-emotional problems are generally conceptualized as internalizing or externalizing problems. Internalizing problems involve depression, anxiety and social withdrawal, whereas externalizing problems are aggression, overactive and impulsive actions (Baker 2006; Baker, Grant and Morlock 2008; Baker et al. 2008). Baker et al. found that children who displayed externalizing behaviour problems and had a close relationship with their teachers achieved better academically. Whereas students who exhibited similar externalizing behaviours and had less warm and close relationships with their teachers struggled in their academic work. This situation was similar to children who showed internalizing behaviour problems. Children who experienced conflicts in their relationships with their teachers performed poorly academically, whereas those children who experienced a positive relationship with their teachers, though they had internalizing behavioural problems, performed well.

Positive teacher-child relationships predict low levels of negative externalizing behaviours and "acted as protective factors, helping to prevent children with high levels of internalizing behaviours in early childhood from developing trajectories of long-term, internalizing behaviour problems" (O'Connor, Dearing and Collins 2012, 122). Rudasill's

(2011) findings gave a positive perspective on teacher-student relationships, which were perceived as negative by the classroom teacher. Teachers exercise more behaviour regulation and provide more emotional support to students by initiating interactions with the students they viewed negatively; this was particularly true at the kindergarten level.

Before starting a new grade, pre-existing levels of student aggression could present challenges for the new teacher. A class characterized by elevated levels of aggression can be very challenging for teachers to forge positive relationships with students and use effective classroom management strategies. Teachers in such circumstances may be prone to use negative control tactics. Relationships between students and teachers are critical for the healthy development of children and the quality of their school experiences, starting at preschool through to subsequent years (Thomas et al. 2011). Hamre and Pianta (2001) noted, "Negativity in kindergarten, marked by conflict and dependency, was related to academic and behavioral outcomes through eighth grade, particularly for children with high levels of behavior problems in kindergarten" (625).

The Influence of Peers

Parents and peers influence and shape children before they enter the school system as they develop. So children do not enter school as blank slates, they carry with them not only their genetical disposition but their experiences with their parents and peers (Collins et al. 2000). Collins et al. (2000) noted that "contemporary models of socialization no longer ask whether children are influenced by parents or peers. Today, socialization researchers develop and test models that examine how parents and peers exert conjoint influence on the developing child" (227). Socialization begins at home with parents. So, parents play a significant role in determining the timing for entry of the child into interaction with peers. They also determine the nature and frequency of that interaction and the types of activities that will be involved in the interaction. While parents are influencing the children's experiences with their peers, the peers, in turn, are impacting the parent-child relationship which further adjusts the children's relationships with their peers. A positive peer relationship is vital as it allows the child to develop social skills, gain social support, and develop healthy self-identity (Parke et al. 2002; Ladd and Pettit 2002; Rose-Krasnor et al. 1996).

Studies on child-parent attachments provide evidence that quality parent-child relationships influence the quality of children's relationships with their peers (Rose-Krasnor et al. 1996; Cassidy et al. 1996; Pallini et al. 2014). Cassidy et al.'s (1996) study involved sixty pre-schoolers who were assessed at fifteen to eighteen months old, using Ainsworth's Strange Situation procedures (see page 29 in chapter 2), and again pre-schoolers at three and a half years for mother-and-peer representation. The results revealed a positive link between children with secured attachment and positive peer representation. The researchers read three stories, "in which a peer with ambiguous intent caused a negative event" (892). The children were asked to pretend that they were the child in the story. Then they were asked questions about the scenarios. Responses to each question were coded as a positive representation or negative representation. Following this set of questions, the children were asked one question concerning their mother: "What did your mother say to you after this happened?" Again, the responses were coded and compared to the first set of questions, and the results from Ainsworth's Strange Situation procedures. Children's daily experiences with parents are critical in understanding their relationships with their peers (Cassidy et al. 1996). At the core of Cassidy et al.'s study was the connection between attachment, representation of parents, and representation of peer relationships. The premise is that children's relationship with their parents influences their actions and relationships with peers. Cassidy et al. concluded that "children who had securely attached and children who had been insecure ambivalent have more positive representations than children who had been insecure-avoidant" (895).

A child has the confidence to explore unfamiliar social environments and enjoy positive interactions with others when a child experience secured attachment. Secured attachment is closely associated with high levels of social competence. Rose-Krasnor et al.'s findings, using a sample of 111 four-year-olds and their mothers, linked secure attachments to children's social engagement competence. The link between attachment and peer relations strengthens as children get older (Schneider, Atkinson and Tardif 2001). Schneider, Atkinson and Tardiff's results show a larger effect size for older participants who were eight years old. This, they suggest, results from children's maturity in social competencies, such as conflict resolution and intimacy. Pallini et al. (2014), following a meta-analysis of literature on early parent attachment and peer relations, gave further confirmation to the above findings when they stated, "This bolsters the contention that early child-parent bonds are related to children's subsequent relationships with peers" (121). Generally, secured attachment develops children's interactive skills and social understanding skills that guard against alienation from their peers and poor peer relationships.

Insecured attachment will generally lead to insecure relationships with peers. These insecure relationships sometimes lead to peer rejection. Peer rejection deprives the rejected children of peer socialization experiences that help to build adaptive social skills and sensitivity to others. Negative peer experiences, including victimization, can lead to the rejected child being involved in deviant behaviours and associating with deviant peers (Rose-Krasnor et al. 1996; Cassidy et al. 1996; Parker et al. 2006; Pallini et al. 2014).

Social and developmental psychologists agree that the classroom and school represent an important context for socialization and the development of certain social skills. The school context continues the socialization with peers and the development of social competences. The teacher-child relationship predicts certain features of social relations with peers. The more secure children feel with their teachers, the more competent they are in their relationship with their peers. Wong's (2017) longitudinal study traced problem behaviours, such as aggressive behaviour in children, as they transitioned from preschool to school. Wong found that most six-year-old children depended on their own efforts to solve dilemmas caused by peers' aggressive behaviours (for example, they would ask the aggressor to stop his or her pursuit). Fewer children in this study sought social support from the teacher; some of the children felt that teachers could not help and that they should solve their problems independently. Wong reported that while 30–40 per cent of the children, after transitioning to school, requested help from teachers, none of the children reported asking peers for support. The researcher speculated that one reason for this could be that the children considered the teachers more competent than their peers in protecting them from peer aggression.

A child's relationship with adults (teachers and parents) influences the quality of the relationship the child will have with his or her peers at school. How teachers respond to behavioural problems can escalate or decrease the intensity of the behaviour. The influence of the parents on children extends far beyond the periphery of the home into the school environment. A child's experience with parents can nurture the development of social skills and prosocial behaviours. Children who have negative experiences with their parents are likely to have poor relationships with peers at school. When children are young, especially at the early childhood stage of development, adults tend not to be concerned about their young children's relationships with other children. As adults, we only become concerned with bloody noses or chronic friendlessness (Hartup and Moore 1990). Peer culture can be so intensely negative that longitudinal studies have revealed the long-lasting impact that such culture can have on children as they transition into adulthood. Children who are high in negative reactivity and shy in temperament tend to experience rejection from their peers as early as elementary schooling. Chapell et al. (2006) findings revealed that among their 119 participants, there was evidence of continuity of the effects of bullying from elementary school to high school and college; the victims of bullying continued to be victims as they transitioned to adulthood. Storey and Slaby (2013) warned that as adults, we have a responsibility to address the problem of bullying because unaddressed, it can continue across the development span, bullies continue to bully, and victims continue to be victims if there is no intervention. Shy children tend to be passive and submissive to their bullies. They lack the skills of assertiveness that will enable them to establish healthy boundaries with their peers; they lack the capacity to say "No" or "stop that". Bullied children prefer to play alone because the challenges of playing with others far outweigh the benefits. On the other hand, children with high negative reactivity tend to respond to bullies with aggression. When bullied, they tend to fight back physically and verbally (Storey and Slaby 2013). For the most part, these children desire to interact with their peers but lack the necessary social skills to initiate and maintain the interactions.

The Influence of Temperament in Teacher-student Interactions

The goodness of fit theory purports that the ideal classroom situation is synchrony between temperament and the environment during the development of a child. In the goodness of fit theory, there is a reciprocal relationship between individuals and their environment. Such relationships suggest that both the individuals and the environment are causing changes in each other. Several studies revealed that teachers' interactions and bond with children are somewhat affected by both the child's and the teacher's temperaments (Thomas and Chess 1977; Coplan et al. 2011; Oren and Jones 2009). Therefore, teachers need to consider how the interaction between their temperament and the students' temperaments are impacting the classroom environment.

The different temperaments of children solicit different responses from teachers. Coplan et al.'s (2011) study revealed that teachers were more likely to respond to exuberant, talkative children with high-powered measures (such as the use of punishment, direct intervention to alter behaviour and having the child make amends) than social learning strategies (such as the use of concrete reinforcements, verbal encouragement or praise, and modelling appropriate behaviours). Teachers in Coplan et al.'s study also felt that shyness is a problem behaviour. For both temperaments, the teachers felt that these characteristics were changeable, and their goal as teachers was to use disciplinary strategies to bring about the change necessary by treating such characteristics as disruptive behaviour in the classroom. In this study, teachers believe that "exuberant children might display greater academic difficulties than do average children, although not as many difficulties as do shy children" (Coplan et al. 2011, 947). On the other hand, Oren and Jones found that children with high negative reactivity (when frustrated children with high reactivity tend to overact and become overly upset) had a positive and high correlation with conflict in the relationship between teacher and students. Again, similar to Coplan et al., Oren and Jones found that some teachers did not empathize with shy children and "lacked the necessary knowledge to deal with or encourage a shy child" (129).

How teachers treat individual children in the classroom affects the classroom environment, which ultimately influences their relationship with the children. Teachers' response to others affects children differently depending on the child's temperament. Bassett et al. (2017) examined temperamental surgency in the classroom. Surgency is "associated with an approach/withdraw tendency to a novel situation, energy activation and sociability" (Bassett et al. 2017, 5). Low surgency children are shy and anxious about meeting new people and attending new events in the environment. In other words, they are cautious and shy in their behaviour. High surgency, on the other hand, are friendly and enjoy social interactions with their peers and teachers. Bassett's study revealed that low surgency children compared to high surgency children were more sensitive to teachers' reactions, whether such reactions were negative or positive, "low-surgency children, that is shy and withdrawn, showed a significant negative relation between teacher unsupportive reactions and emotionally negative/aggressive behaviors" (10). Low surgency students talk less but observe more; as such, teachers need to be aware that other children are observing their reaction to their classmates and are impacted by their behaviour towards the other children. For example, if a teacher shows empathetic reactions by acknowledging a child's frustration for not getting the favourite toy, then the teacher is not only helping the child to reduce the frustration but also modelling empathic behaviours to other children in the classroom (Bassett et al. 2017). Teachers' behaviour can create a secure or an insecure environment for children with a certain temperament.

Students' success in school has been linked to individual differences in reactivity and regulation. The following dimensions are grouped under reactivity, surgency-extraversion (SU) and negative affect (NA). At the same time, effortful control (EC) describes individual differences in self-regulation, including inhibitory control and goal-oriented regulation of attention and activation (Checa and Abundis-Gutierrez 2017). Children in early elementary school (i.e., kindergarten to third grade) who adults rate as having high levels of self-regulation or effortful control experience high academic achievement and are well adjusted to the school environment. These children are mildly frustrated when doing their academic tasks and continue to achieve academically at relatively high levels in middle school or high school. Students with task persistent temperament can and will remain on a task until the goal is achieved (Valiente et al. 2011; Sanchez-Perez et al. 2015). In other words, such children with a high level of effortful control are likely to be successful academically than children with low levels of effort control. Children high in effort control also liked school and forge better relationships with peers (Valiente et al. 2007; Morris et al. 2013). The literature points to the need for schools to implement strategies that can be implemented to help improve children who are low in effortful control. It is imperative that teachers understand children's temperaments to plan and implement ways to help children manage their negative reactivity or improve their task persistence. This can only happen when educators understand individuals' characteristically differences.

Summary

The chapter explored the role of the teacher-student relationship in influencing students' behaviour in the classroom. We also discussed the influence of relationship with peers and how parents influence such a relationship and ultimately behaviour in the school context. Finally, in this chapter, we discussed the interaction of teachers and students' temperaments in the classroom. Some studies show that children's problem behaviours can be aggravated by teacher-student relationship. Frustrated teachers rely on ineffective and negative behavioural management strategies such as threats, nags and authoritarian measures to get compliance, whereas a positive relationship between teachers and students predict low levels of behavioural problems. In such relationships, teachers give more emotional support to students. Other studies show that teachers who perceived their relationship with students to be negative will initiate interactions with students and provide more emotional support to such students.

Before students enter school, their peers and parents influence their early development. Studies revealed that children who have secure attachment with their parents go on to have a positive relationship with their peers. On the other hand, insecure attachment leads to a negative relationship with peers. Children's daily experiences with their parents are very important in understanding their experiences with their peers. It is important to note that negative relationship with peers deprives individuals of developing the adaptive social skills and sensitivity to others.

Studies revealed that there are children with high levels of negative reaction or shyness who solicit punitive measures from teachers. Children with withdrawn temperament tend not to talk but are more likely to be very observant. They draw conclusions about the environment from their observation of how the teacher responds and treat other children in the classroom. The chapter concluded that teachers' behaviours create the classroom environment, and this is particularly true at the kindergarten level.

4. Fostering Development of Jamaican Children

Behavioural problems in the classroom have many expressions; in Jamaica, aggression is a significant problem. Children are both perpetrators and victims of violence and aggression in Jamaica. According to Harriott and Jones (2016), notwithstanding the general decline in major crime since 2009, Jamaican children are still on a dangerous pathway of violence and aggression; they are both victims and perpetrators of crime and violence. Children experience aggression from various sources – the community, home, school and their peers (Henningham-Baker, Meeks-Gardner, Chang and Walker 2009; Harriott and Jones 2016). Children are also harshly disciplined by parents who engage in authoritarian childrearing practices (McClowry and Spellman 2016; Harriott and Jones 2016). Authoritarian parents tend to exercise control over children's attitudes and behaviours. Such parents value obedience and favour punitive measures (Baumrind 1966).

Jamaican parents exert physical violence on their children through the use of corporal punishment (Fernald and Meeks-Gardner 2003; Brown and Johnson 2008; The Jamaican Reproductive Survey 2008 [2010]); Harriot and Jones 2016). Fernald and Meeks-Gardner (2003) found that 75 per cent of the children (77 of 103) participating in their study reported that their parents used corporal punishment to discipline them. The students responded to the question, "What happens if you get into trouble at home?" by voicing the following:

> My mother will beat me and send me to my bed. (female)

> My mother beat we or punish we. (male)

> Mother will beat you and cuss you. (female)

> My mother cuss me and lick [hit] me with her hand. (male)

> My mother beat me. And send me to mi [my] bed. (female)

> My mother will beat me. And me have to run. I have to hide. (male)

In one extreme example, a child reported:

> My mother beat me. And kick me. And fling stone after me. Turn me upside down and beat me. And run me down with stone. And lick me up with stick. She cook and didn't give me any. (male) (131)

The Reproductive Health Survey Jamaica (2010) reported that approximately 61.2 per cent of the female participants in the survey stated that they had been slapped, kicked, shoved and hit by a parent or stepparent before the age of fifteen. Similarly, 57.6 per cent of Jamaican males who participated in the survey reported that before the age of fifteen years they experienced physical abuse from parents or stepparents. Women who felt that physical punishment was the most effective way to discipline a child, experienced physical punishment and witnessed abuse compared with women who were not exposed to aggression (Reproductive Health Survey Jamaica 2010). Parents' authoritarian disposition in childrearing practices were also confirmed by Brown and Johnson (2008), who reported that the majority of parents they interviewed believed in and valued obedience and manners and defended corporal punishment. According to Brown and Johnson, this was especially true in under-resourced communities. Such parents felt that it was their duty to develop resilience in their children, *who must grow up tough* to survive the harsh reality of poverty. Jamaican parents justify and defend authoritarian childrearing practices, including the use of punitive measures to improve their children's conduct and give them opportunities in life. The excessively harsh discipline most times do not lead to the expected outcome. Instead, children run away from home and in most cases, join street gangs (Harriott and Jones 2016). Children who are exposed to high levels of violence in their communities tend to exhibit aggressive or delinquent behaviours (Gilede 2012; Guerra, Huesmann and Spindler 2003). Jamaican children are often exposed to violence either as victims or witnesses (Samms-Vaughan, Jackson and Ashley 2005; Harriott and Jones 2016; The Reproductive Health Survey Jamaica 2010).

In regard to schools, Fernald and Meeks-Gardner (2003) reported that children said that they were punished by teachers who beat them and put them in a dark room, and "sometimes they had to stand out in the sun with their hands atop their heads," or they were beaten in front of their peers. One female student reinforced the teachers' discipline strategy by describing her encounter as follow: "Sometimes she beat us, and sometimes she gives us books, heavy books to put on your head to punish you" (133). Pottinger and Nelson (as cited in Henningham-Baker et al. 2009) reported that their study, involving seventy-four primary schoolteachers from four schools in the capital of Jamaica, revealed that 80 per cent of the participating teachers used corporal punishment as a means of punishment.

Parental aggression in the form of corporal punishment often results in children displaying aggressive behaviours (Yaros, Lochman and Wells 2016). Corporal punishment is a form of discipline that is used widely in Jamaica and the Caribbean. Corporal punishment is not illegal, but it is discouraged by the Ministry of Education in Jamaica. However, despite the ministry's stance, there is a strong endorsement of the use of corporal punishment among parents and teachers (Henningham-Baker et al.; Walker 2009).

Peer bullying is one of the risk factors for children developing aggressive behaviours as they mature and, in some cases, children experience mental health and substance abuse issues (Ybrandt and Armelius 2010; Moore et al. 2014; Arseneault et al. 2006). Moore et al. (2014) in a longitudinal study involving 1,590 adolescents found that there was a strong relationship between peer aggression and later mental health and substance abuse problems. Arseneault et al. (2006) carried out a study that involved children who had experienced bullying when they were five and seven years. Arseneault et al. (2006) concluded that young children who experienced bullying were more likely to be maladjusted to school during the first years of their schooling. Their findings also revealed that children who were victims of bullying in the early developmental stage (between the ages of five and seven years) had more internalizing problems compared to children who did not experience bullying. Also, the children who were bullied early in life when compared to the children who did not experience bullying had less prosocial behaviour. Their teachers also reported that they were less happy.

In Jamaica, Fernald and Meeks-Gardner (2003) reported that the children in their study who attended schools in under-resourced communities were often involved in bullying and other forms of peer victimization. Henningham-Baker et al. (2009) found the aggression was prevalent in the participating primary schools. Their study revealed that only 29 per cent of the students reported that they were not exposed to aggression in the participating schools.

Peer aggression involved being threatened by other children and being involved in fights. Henningham-Baker et al. (2009) concluded that a large portion of Jamaican children is exposed to aggression among peers, especially in government primary schools in urban areas. Henningham-Baker et al. (2009) also felt that there is an urgent need to implement validated violence prevention programs on a school-wide basis within these urban schools. Several other experts (Arseneault et al. 2006; Meeks-Gardner et al. 2003; Henningham-Baker et al., 2009) have called for early prevention programmes to reduce aggression and violence in schools.

The Early Childhood Education Landscape in Jamaica

Early childhood education started in Jamaica with Dudley Ransford Brandyce Grant, otherwise known as DRB Grant, the father of early childhood education. In 1963, Dudley Ransford Brandyce Grant, a lecturer and member of the academic staff of the Institute of Education, School of Education, the University of the West Indies, Mona, conducted academic research in the field of teacher education. He taught courses for infant schoolteachers and developed and introduced innovative teacher-training methods. While at the Institute of Education in 1966, DRB Grant played a significant role in implementing the Project for Early Childhood Education (PECE), financed by the Bernard van Leer Foundation. He was responsible for managing and organizing the Centre for Early Childhood Education (CE).

The PECE was initially a three-year experimental project. The project was successful and eventually evolved into the Ministry of Education's Early Childhood Programme that started in the 1970s, following the success of the early childhood education project financed by the Bernard van Leer Foundation (National Library of Jamaica, n.d.). A World Bank Report (n.d.) noted: Jamaica has a notably extensive legal and instrumental framework for early childhood education, including a draft National Plan of Action for Early Childhood Education, an Early Childhood Commission, and an Early Childhood Policy. The legislative framework comprises the Early Childhood Commission Act of 2004 and the Early Childhood Act and Regulations enforced in 2005. These are bolstered by the broader Child Care and Protection Act of March 2004 (15).

The 2003 Early Childhood Commission Act launched the Early Childhood Commission (ECC). ECC activities are guided by The Jamaica Early Childhood Curriculum for Children, from birth to five years, which was developed in 2008. Today, the ECC is responsible for approximately twenty-eight hundred early childhood institutions in Jamaica (nursery, preschool and kindergarten). Children enter nursery and preschool from as early as three months. The age range for formal early childhood education is three to five years (Caribbean Policy Research Institute [CAPRI] 2012). Early education is not mandatory in Jamaica (CAPRI 2012). However, Jamaica experiences high levels of enrolment for children three to five years old. CAPRI (2012) reported that 99 per cent of the children in this age group are registered in schools. According to CAPRI (2012), international rates are lower, ranging from 74 per cent to 80 per cent.

Jamaica is fully on board with early intervention. The Education Transformation Project in early 2005, the Parenting Support Commission and the development of a National Parenting Policy were tabled under the leadership of the ECC (Early Childhood Commission). In the conclusion of the World Bank Report (n.d.), it was noted that Jamaica has a well-written institutional, legal and policy framework in place to guide the relevant institutions (health, housing and education). Despite the early start for children in schooling, our education – both academically and socially still faces a severe crisis. CAPRI's (2012) report noted:

> Evidence suggests that skills in math are even weaker. In 2009, Jamaica conducted its first national numeracy assessment of fourth graders. Data show that less than half (45%) of the students mastered the skills set, which includes "number representation and number operations; decimals and fractions; measurement; geometry; algebra; statistics and probability." Performance improved slightly in 2011, moving to 49%, but is still far from satisfactory. Some educators argue that the deficiency in the education system starts at the early childhood level. (17)

Oscar van Leer, son of the founder of the Bernard van Leer Foundation, is noted for saying that "all children should be able to achieve the greatest possible realization of innate intellectual potential". Our innate intellectual property is not independent of our social, psychological and socio-emotional state. Vygotsky observed that there is a complex interdependency among the physical, technological, socio-economical and intellectual environments in determining the possibilities of an individual (van der Veer 2007). We are products not only of our genes but also of our environment. Bronfenbrenner's (1974) ecological theory illustrates that the complexity of the child's environment and its interaction with the developing child give insights into the child's characteristics. Bronfenbrenner (1974) promoted early intervention and the critical role of parents in intervention programmes that target children. He felt that the family is so important to society that parenting should be taught to youngsters before they become parents; they should be taught while at school. However, failing this, parents must be the primary target of any intervention. Effective intervention must strengthen bonding between parents and child. Parents are the primary agents in the child's development. Bronfenbrenner noted, "a program which places the parent in a subordinate role, dependent on the expert, is not likely to be effective in the long run" (56). The school, which is also part of the intimate layer in Bronfenbrenner's ecological theory, is an essential context for intervention as well. Several writers noted that the school, as an agent of socialization, has the potential to influence the socialization of aggression (Thomas, Bierman and Powers 2011). In Jamaica, there have been several interventions aimed to address behavioural problems, such as the high levels of violence and aggression in the schools. Two large projects – Peace and Love in Schools (PALS) and Change from Within – have been implemented for several years, to train young Jamaicans in good conflict management skills.

Change from Within

The Change from Within programme in Jamaica was developed by the late Sir Philip Sherlock, a former vice-chancellor of the University of the West Indies. At the core of *Change from within* is restorative justice circles for conflict resolution. The programme addressed the rising levels of aggression and violence in society and targeted transforming school cultures and "bringing about positive qualitative and quantitative changes concerning the esteem and involvement of school stakeholders, leadership skills amongst principal, teachers, and students, academic performance" (Ferguson, Samuels and Gordon 2018, 10). There are eight core principles of Change from Within are (1) empowering school leaders, (2) working with existing good practices, (3) utilizing new pedagogies, (4) mentoring at all levels (teachers, school leaders, children), (5) involving parents and the wider community, (6) involving children in decision making, (7) training staff and students and (8) offering a shared circle of support. The programme was implemented in thirty-six schools by 2007 (Ferguson and Chevannes 2018).

Restorative justice focuses on repairing the harm caused by deviant behaviour while holding the wrongdoer responsible for his or her actions. The intervention by providing an opportunity for the parties, the victim and the offender to come together seeks a resolution that leads to healing, reparation and reintegration and prevents future harm (Ferguson and Chevannes 2018). Restorative justice as an alternative to using punitive measures for disciplining children in the classroom aims at building communities in the classrooms. These communities are supported by "clear agreements, authentic communication, and specific tools to bring issues and conflicts forward in a helpful way" (6). Restorative justice allows for safer schools and adds quality to the social and emotional development of participants. While the teacher was originally in charge of behavioural management, there is a shift from the teacher to a more team effort with the students involved and there is now a shared responsibility for behaviour in the classroom. Both teachers and students take responsibility for minimizing problem behaviours. There are several principles for establishing dialogue using restorative justice. However, the following are examples of those principles:

- At the beginning, students sit in a circle (gives a stronger sense of community). "A talk tool is used, which is passed to each student just before he or she starts talking. In this way, every child will know that they have a chance to put their voice in the center" (Amos Clifford, Center for Restorative Process, n.d., 10). Circle members are reminded to respect each person who is talking by the "talking piece defenders" (these are circle members who are assigned the role of defenders).
- The circle keeper can ask questions about building and maintaining a community. There are also "restorative questions". These questions are used to guide dialogue "leading to understanding the consequences of harmful behaviour, and agreement about how to remove those harms" (Amos Clifford, Center for Restorative Process, n.d., 12). Closure questions invite circle members to reflect on what happened in the circle.

The Restorative Justice circle allows for the sustainable development of values and healthy behaviour by developing students' conflict management and enhancing the interpersonal skills by students learning how to work together.

Peace and Love in Society (PALS)

PALS began in 1994 as Peace and Love in Schools and was renamed Peace and Love in Society in 2004. The goal of PALS is to influence positive change in behaviour by teaching dispute resolution techniques. The programme offers eighteen different programmes to schools in the form of workshops. Three of the eighteen programmes are Managing Conflict and Violence in Schools, Creating and Nurturing the School Climate and Classroom Management.

Managing Conflict and Violence in Schools: This workshop guides participants in understanding, managing and solving the conflict. Participants gain knowledge in skills in understanding and managing anger, and they are exposed to the concept of emotional intelligence. Their assertive, negotiation and communication skills are enhanced. Participants learn the importance of creating a community of respect, tolerance, equality and justice.

Creating and Nurturing the School: According to PALS, culture concerns how the school gets work done and the emotional atmosphere generated in the process. The programme involves educators gaining an understanding of conflict in the classroom. In so doing, participants examine the challenges that students face; examine successful behaviours of successful children; and assist teachers in identifying strategies and positive attitudes in creating a friendly classroom.

Classroom Management: PALS classroom management programme targets instructional management skills. Teachers acquiring these skills will be better able to manage students on task behaviours that allow the students to be actively engaged during the teaching-learning process. Teachers examine the role of classroom rules and how to formulate and enforce the regulations with practical consequences (see the PALS website).

While Change from Within and PALS targeted high schools in Jamaica, the early childhood level lacked comprehensive programmes that focused on training children from early in their development in conflict management skills and enhancing teachers' and parents' disciplining skills geared towards understanding the child and using less punitive measures. Henningham-Baker et al. (2009) piloted the Incredible Years (IY) Teacher Training Programme, which targeted early childhood institutions and exposed children from an early age. The IY programme involved seven units that were delivered for the entire school year. The programme goals were "(i) learning school rules; (ii) learning how to do your best in school; (iii) understanding and detecting feelings; (iv) problem-solving skills; (v) anger management; (vi) learning how to be friendly; and (vii) learning how to talk with friends" (4). These programmes and interventions have continued to have an impact on the levels of aggression among children.

Before 2013, no intervention focused on helping parents and teachers to appreciate personality differences in children and assist children in understanding and accepting their own and peers' uniqueness as individuals. INSIGHTS into Children's Temperament was developed by Sandee McClowry, a professor from New York University. The programme was implemented in Jamaica in 2013. INSIGHTS is an evidence-based, comprehensive intervention that enhances the social-emotional development and academic learning of young children and the behaviour management skills of their parents and teachers.

The INSIGHTS into Children's temperament programme is an evidence-based intervention that provides parents and teachers with child behaviour management strategies tailored to fit different children's personality styles. Children also learn problem-solving strategies to resolve dilemmas with parents, teachers and peers. There are growing concerns about problem behaviours among students in the preschool and primary school level as such behaviours impact children's relationships with their teachers, parents and peers. If these problem behaviours are not dealt with early in a child's life, they can become ingrained in an unwillingness to display socially acceptable behaviour. INSIGHTS' programme addresses the day-to-day disciplinary problems familiar to most parents and teachers.

Students' behaviour problems have for years been a major concern of teachers, administrators and parents (McClowry et al. 2010; Masten et al. 2005). Over time, behaviour problems trigger a cascade of negative functioning, which spills over into other negative behaviours as the child develops (Masten et al., 2005). Such progression of behaviour problems, if there is no early intervention, can have "diffusing effects" over time (Masten et al. 2005). Several studies have shown that problem behaviours can have a pathway of development from early in a child's development. Such development can lead to more behaviour and academic problems as individuals' development progresses (Tremblay, Gerald and Petitclerc 2008). These problem behaviours in the classroom can range from excessive movement, talking without permission, to fighting, disrespecting teachers, bullying and vandalism (Harrison et al. 2012). Problem behaviours if left without intervention can escalate over time and negatively affect not only the involved students but also their peers. This is particularly true for preschool and elementary children who can experience long-term benefits from early intervention (Tremblay et al. 2008; Piquero et al. (2009).

The INSIGHTS programme is underpinned by Goodness of Fit Model and the Diathesis-Stress Model as applied to temperament theory by Martin (1994) and McClowry (2014). These models were discussed earlier, along with the attachment theory, which give insights into how the quality of emotional bonding from birth can influence children's behaviours. The programme provides participants with strategies to enhance teachers' and parents' confidence and skills when managing daily disciplinary issues.

Insights into Children's Temperaments intervention is an evidence-based intervention involving the synchronous action of the teacher, parent and classroom programme working to support children's social-emotional development and academic learning. The programme provides parents and teachers with child behaviour management strategies which are tailored to fit children's personality types and enhance the children's self-regulation through strengthening their empathy and problem-solving skills. INSIGHTS intervention helps children, from as early as five years old, to solve dilemmas and to celebrate differences among each other. In learning how to solve dilemmas, the programme equips students with conflict management strategies from an early age.

INSIGHTS is a comprehensive programme with components which include teachers, parents and children. The conceptualization of INSIGHTS is based on temperament theories which provide a framework for the building blocks of the programme. The overarching aim of INSIGHTS is to improve the fit of the child's temperament with the environment in which the child is being nurtured and scaffolded. According to McClowry et al. (2010), when goodness-of-fit is achieved "competent behaviors can be expected" (25); however, "if there is poorness-of-fit, maladaptive behavior is more likely to result" (25). Hence the intervention provides parents and teachers with child behaviour management strategies tailored to fit different children's temperaments. Children also learn problem-solving strategies to resolve dilemmas with parents, teachers and peers. With temperament (personality) theory as its foundation, INSIGHTS provides parents and teachers with a framework for appreciating children's individual differences. INSIGHTS programme assists parents and teachers with replacing negative patterns of interaction and harsh disciplinary practices with responsive ones that match a child's temperament. The programme enhances children's self-regulation by strengthening their empathy and problem-solving skills (INSIGHTS Manual).

The INSIGHTS Intervention Curriculum: Parent and Teacher Sessions

Parents learn to recognize or identify the qualities and constraints of children's behaviours that are unique to their temperaments. Teachers and parents are guided in how to reframe or reassess and re-describe their understanding of their children's temperaments and behaviours, thereby understanding the children's strengths and constraints (McClowry et al. 2010). According to McClowry et al., teachers and parents also "learn that while temperament is not amenable to change, their responses are and these responses greatly influence a child's behavior" (25).

Both the parents and teachers participate in ten weekly sessions which are held in separate venue and at different times. The content of the teacher-and-parent programme is delivered by a facilitator who uses a structured curriculum. The curriculum includes didactic content, professionally produced vignettes, handouts, group activities and individual assignments. The puppets exemplify the different temperaments of school-aged children as follows: Coretta the Cautious (cautious/slow to warm), Gregory the Grumpy (high maintenance), Fredrico the Friendly (social/eager to try) and Hilary the Hard Worker (industrious).

Coretta the Cautious (cautious/slow to warm)

Gregory the Grumpy (high maintenance)

Fredrico the Friendly (social/eager to Try)

Hilary the Hard Worker (industrious)

There are dimensions to each temperament. The child who is high on withdrawal is slow to warm up. Children with this temperament are reluctant to try new experiences. However, over time, with the right support, the individuals learn to manage their shyness and feel more comfortable to experience new situations. Children who are classified as grumpy are high on negative reactivity but low in task persistence and high on activity. According to McClowry, children who are grumpy are aware of the negative reaction of their temperament and that some children and adults find them annoying. Therefore, these children need their parents' and teachers' assistance in developing the controls necessary to enhance their social interactions. Friendly children are low on withdrawal. They are eager to meet new people and experience new situations. Parents are often concerned about the safety of friendly children. Also, because they are so eager to please, they are not usually assertive. The final temperament is the hard worker. Children who are classified as hard workers are low in negative reactivity, high in task persistence and low in activity. Such individuals are industrious. These students also desire to please adults and therefore need help to be assertive (of differing from the adults).

Parents and teachers in their separate sessions are introduced to the concept that temperament influences a child's behaviour and emotional reactions. Temperament does not mean the same thing as "temper" or "temper tantrum", nor does it mean bad behaviour. It is, instead, a style of behaviour and a consistent way of viewing the world. Temperament refers to the normal variations we see in children. Consequently, there are no good and bad temperaments. Each type of temperament has strengths, but some tendencies cause parents and teachers to be concerned (INSIGHTS Manual, 4). The children are also introduced to the concept via audio-visual productions.

Phases of the INSIGHTS Programme: Summary of the Programme's Key Principles

Part 1: The 3 Rs of Child Management: Recognize, Reframe and Respond

Session 1: Recognizing Child Temperament: At the beginning of the programme, facilitators welcome participants and allow each participant to introduce him or herself and expectations of the programme. The facilitator then gives an overview of the programme and emphasizes the importance of maintaining trust in the programme by keeping the discussions confidential. The content of session one includes a discussion of the following concepts of temperament: its biological basis, resistance to modification, manifestation in situations involving stress and change, and relationship to goodness-of-fit. Vignettes demonstrating the four dimensions of school-age temperaments are shown. Participants are asked to observe the children during the week for expressions of temperament.

Session 2: Reframing Child Temperament: The facilitator then discusses the temperament profile with the participants. The strengths and concerns of each specific temperament are highlighted. For example, a child who is low maintenance is task persistent and spends a long time doing schoolwork or puzzles. The adults in this child's life may be concerned about the lack of assertiveness. Participants are asked to observe their children's behaviour and their own response to a situation that occurs during the week.

Session 3: Parent and Teacher Responses: Teachers and parents are guided in assessing their responses and ways of selecting the most appropriate response. The video vignettes in this session demonstrate how parent or teacher responses influence the quality of the adult/child interactions.

Teachers and parents are shown different scenarios using visuals and required to assess all responses to each of these scenarios by deciding if the scenarios are optimal, adequate or counterproductive. The importance of how the adult responds and the message sent in each response is discussed.

Part 2: Gaining compliance.

Session 4: Gaining Control: This session emphasizes how parents or teachers gain compliance through effective behavioural management strategies. Adults are taught how to design and implement contracts for behaviours that the child finds hard to change. The contract is between the adult and the child, based on agreed consequences. During the intervention, the INSIGHTS facilitators emphasize that acceptance of a child's temperament does not mean permissiveness (McClowry et al. 2010). Teachers and parents are encouraged to match as much as possible behavioural strategies to the child's temperament. INSIGHTS focuses on strategies that help children to make independent decisions confidently. Homework includes implementing the contract and reporting results in subsequent sessions

Session 5: Fostering Competencies: This session introduces social competencies that enhance relationships and collaboration. The following strategies are highlighted during the session: listening, empathy, giving recognition, assertiveness and cooperation. This session provides additional strategies that "support children in becoming more competent when encountering temperamentally challenging situations" (McClowry et al. 2010, 25). Parents and teachers are guided on how to scaffold or stretch a child. The participants must assess the situation and decide if the child needs guided support. The adults are exposed to strategies that can gently be utilized to stretch the child emotionally and, ultimately, to influence his/her behaviour positively. Over time, the child is expected, through these stretching strategies, to develop his/her own self-regulatory competence.

Session 6: More Competencies: Strategies (problem-solving, controlling one's temper and conflict resolution) relevant to other social competencies are described and discussed. Participants are encouraged to develop contracts with themselves and to collaborate with their child's class on a group project.

Session 7: Disciplining School-aged Children: The general principles of discipline are discussed in this session. Adults are assisted in developing guidelines for handling non-compliance and disrespect. Children's temperaments are also further discussed.

Session 8: Parents and Teachers Are People, Too: Adults are encouraged to take care of themselves. Strategies on how parents can meet the needs of children while caring for their own needs are discussed. For example, parents are encouraged to take a time-out, which allows them to cool down, think and relax.

Session 9: Fostering Independence and Responsibility: In this session, the facilitator explains strategies that are likely to foster independence and responsibility. The facilitator also explores developmentally appropriate behaviours with the adults. Also, the facilitator starts reviewing sessions 1–3.

Part 3: Summary
Session 10: Putting It All Together: Sessions 4–8 are reviewed in this session, and more complex situations concerning students' behaviour are explored. Completion certificates are distributed to parents, teachers and children at the end of this session.

The INSIGHTS Intervention Curriculum: Children Sessions

In the classroom programme, the facilitator uses puppets to train the children in resolving daily dilemmas. Each classroom teacher reinforces these principles throughout the week following each session. The children's sessions are ten weekly lessons designed for forty-five minutes. Children are introduced to the four puppets that represent the different temperaments (Gregory the Grumpy, Frederic the Friendly, Coretta the Cautious and Hilary the Hard Worker). They learn the similarities and differences between individuals based on their temperaments. Children are guided (using the video vignettes) in a discussion of situations and activities that are easy and challenging for each temperament. During the second half of the programme, children are guided into solving dilemmas they are likely to experience in their daily lives. During these sessions, the facilitators ask students to generate a list of their own problem situations or activities (dilemmas). The children then work together through role play with the puppets to apply the process they learn in INSIGHTS to resolve these problem situations or activities. They are also taught to solve dilemmas as they interact with each other. A predominant principle session is acceptance of self and others. Each session ends with the song "I'm Unique. You're Unique". A facilitator or a classroom teacher can implement INSIGHTS Children's sessions. Children have a reprise attached to their sessions – I'm unique. You're unique.

Evidence of INSIGHTS' Effectiveness

Clinical trials revealed that INSIGHTS enhanced teacher efficacy in managing students' disruptive behaviour in inner-city primary schools (McClowry et al. 2010), and INSIGHTS aided teachers in improving the goodness-of-fit between a child's temperament and the academic learning context (McCornick et al. 2015). A group-randomized trial that tested the efficacy of

INSIGHTS reported an increase in "the academic achievement and sustained attention and reducing the disruptive behaviour problems of low-income kindergarten and 1st grade children" (O'Connor et al. 2014a, 1156). The researchers also reported that children who participated in the INSIGHTS intervention experienced increased performance in Mathematics and Reading achievement and sustained attention compared to children who participated in a supplemental reading programme. In addition, the effects of improved performance in Mathematics and Reading were mediated "through a reduction in behaviour problems and the effects on reading were partially mediated through sustained attention" (1156). Cappella et al. (2015) reported on the efficacy of INSIGHTS in improving teachers' observed practices of emotional support and classroom organization and students' behaviours for the early elementary grades, along with Grade 1. Multilevel random effects models "showed an INSIGHTS main effect on observed teacher practices of emotional support. This effect was magnified in first grade. First-grade INSIGHTS classrooms also had higher teacher practices of classroom organization ..." (217). Cappella et al. concluded that the findings, though modest in some instances, draw attention to the characteristics of INSIGHTS. The programme explicitly teaches the recognition by parents and teachers of individual children's strengths and needs, and the responsibilities of adults to help children with their needs by scaffolding and support of the children for whom they are responsible. The programme challenges teachers and parents to be flexible in their strategies for managing children's negative reactions, which are indications of the "needs" of students. It is important to point out that due to ethical reasons children were not studied directly for behavioural changes but instead, the research relied on the report of the adults.

Summary

In Jamaica, aggression and violence are the major behavioural problems in schools. Children are exposed from very young to violence and aggression. Children are not only victims of aggression but are exposed to adults' treatment of others in an aggressive manner. Children experience aggression from multiple sources – the home, the community and the school. In recognition of the need to start from early in children's development and to provide a healthy environment for growth and maturity, the Jamaican government established the Early Childhood Commission (ECC) in 2003. The ECC became responsible for early childhood institutions ensuring that high standards are upheld and that children are protected from abuse. Due to the problems of aggression and violence in schools, interventions such as Change from within and Peace and Love in the Society (PALS) were developed and implemented, targeting high schools.

In 2009, Henningham-Baker et. al reported on Incredible Years and intervention at the early childhood level. This programme was developed and tested overseas. Henningham-Baker et al. also tested the programme in Jamaica. They reported that the programme targeted children understanding their feelings; learning how to solve problems from early in their daily lives and learning how to talk to friends. In 2013, INSIGHTS into Children's Temperament was introduced in Jamaica as a collaboration between NYU and UWI. This is an evidence-based intervention focused on sensitizing teachers to children's temperaments and gearing from a one-size-fit-all behavioural management strategy to understanding differences in the classroom. INSIGHTS was piloted in Jamaica in the mid-twenties. The following chapters discuss the programme and the issues around parenting and teaching that were revealed based on the assessment of the programme's efficacy.

5. Teachers' Assessment of a Sample of Jamaican Children's Temperament

Though the literature on children's temperament in Jamaica is scanty, it is critical that the training of educators involves their understanding of children's temperament, which focuses on the development of individual differences. Hence, discussing children's temperamental dimensions is a precursor to understanding children's differences in the early childhood classroom, thus allowing teachers to implement more temperamental appropriate practices in the classroom. The majority of children in schools are typical children in that they did well enough to be in regular school and did not need special education assistance (Martin, Lease and Slobodskya 2020). This chapter aims to discuss more in depth the various dimensions of temperament and the implication of these dimensions in the classroom. The discussion includes the temperamental profile of what typical children could look like based on a sample of Jamaican children temperament profiles reported by teachers.

Temperament is "constitutionally based in individual differences, in reactivity, and self-regulation in the domain of affect, activity and attention" (Rothbart and Bates 2006, 100). Constitutionally based means the influence of heredity, maturation and experience in distinguishing an individual's temperamental differences. Reactivity refers to an individuals' (affective, activity and attention) response to internal and external environmental changes (Rothbart 2012, 10; Rothbart and Bates 2006). Self-regulation is the ability to wait for an appropriate time to respond, resist the temptation to lash out at others, be very focused on long-term goals and defer immediate gratifications to achieve future goals. Children with high self-regulation manage distraction well. So self-regulation moderates reactivity (Rothbart and Bates 2006).

Negative Reactivity

Some children are more petulant than others. Their response to life's everyday frustration is generally expressed with more negative emotions than others; they cry, scream and direct verbal aggression at others. Negative reactivity seems to have roots in biology and the nurturing environment children are exposed to during their development. As mentioned earlier, genes such as the dopamine D4 receptor (DRD4) have been associated with aggression (Martin, Lease and Slobodskya 2020). While nature influences the development of negative reactivity, it is important for teachers to note that the nurturing environment created in the classroom influences the levels of negative emotions exhibited by children. Several research findings revealed that children who showed high levels of negative reactivity in their early years could learn or develop regulatory skills that allow them to manage their reactions. For example, Almas et al. (2011) found that at twenty-four months of age children who were categorized as having high levels of negative reactivity displayed dysregulation skills; they were irritable, easily frustrated, angered and sad. The researchers, however, found by the time these infants were thirty-six months of age, their levels of dysregulation lowered across the researchers two assessment points. Almas et al. (2011) concluded, "It seems that, with time, children may learn more positive regulation strategies or behaviours during care, thereby decreasing the levels of aggressive or dysregulated behaviours they initially display in the care setting" (12). Koenen et al. (2019) studied seventy-one teacher-student interactions in a special education institution. The researchers concluded, "Student maladjustment and teachers' depersonalization attitudes were positively associated with activating negative emotions" (37). Koenen et al. (2019) reported that "Our results suggested that these lower quality interactions are associated with more negative emotions including not only activating feelings of irritation but also deactivating feelings of guilt and helplessness. In addition, teachers who were less able to structure their support toward the students and felt less effective in their classroom management appeared also to be less able to regulate their negative emotions" (45).

Koenen et al. (2019) also found that teachers who were burnt out were more vulnerable to negative emotions; such teachers used inadequate coping strategies and tended to activate negative emotions from their children. Dollar et al. (2018), in an earlier study, concluded, "our results provide support for early entry points to teach toddlers, especially those high in anger reactivity, the skills to engage in socially appropriate interactions with classmates and teachers, which may lessen after academic challenges"(1).

Shyness

Shyness is a temperamental trait characterized by an individual being low in approach, fearful, self-conscious, cautious, socially fearful and slow to warm up (Rubin and Copeland 2010; McClowry 2014). Shyness "has been conceptualized as (temperamental) wariness in the face of social novelty and self-conscious behaviour in situations of perceived social evaluation (Rubin and Copland 2010, 9). Self-consciousness is "believing oneself to be the object of others' attention" (Crozier 2010, 42). Crozier (2010) following the conclusions of results from several investigations of shyness in individuals explained, "Shy individuals lack confidence and efficacy about their social interactions. Shy individuals tend to have low self-esteem. They are also motivated to be effective in their self-presentation but doubt their competence to do so. In their tendency to make "stable, internal attributions for their social difficulties—they blame themselves for their predicaments" (Crozier 2010, 44). Some shy individuals engage in self-talk during social interactions that are negative and self-deprecatory. The self-conscious individual views self through the eyes of others; these others can be present or imagined. The *imagined*, for the most part, is based on the shy individual's experiences. The individual becomes a detached observer of the "self" (Crozier 2010). Rochat (2003) referred to the act of self-awareness as metacognitive self-awareness. Crozier noted that self-talks by shy individuals such as "If I say *X*, I might appear foolish or stupid, or other people will think less of me in some way" (46), stretches across cultures. The shy individual's self-monitoring of behaviour, for the most part, takes on a defensive stance in that the aim is to ward off negative outcomes rather than bring about positive ones.

Because shy children are slow to warm up and are high on social withdrawal, they remove themselves from peer interactions. Their removal from peer interactions could be because of fear, anxiety, or emotional dysregulation or could simply be "a non-fearful preference for solitary activities" (Rubin and Copeland 2010, 8). The latter phenomena have not received as much attention in research as the former (Rubin and Copeland 2010). Many studies and attention have been given to children who withdraw from social interaction because of fear and anxiety. Shy children tend to be onlookers (i.e., they watch others but do not join in). Socially withdrawn children are sometimes at risk for rejections from peers and "friendliness that place them at risk for later socioemotional and academic difficulties" (Rubin, Bowker and Gazelle 2010, 131). Shy children can be at risk for experiencing peer rejection, exclusion and victimization (Rubin, Bowker and Gazelle

2010). Conversely, some socially withdrawn children who do not encounter rejection and exclusion from their peers and over time can become less withdrawn and experience fewer adjustment problems. Some factors that help buffer shy, withdrawn children from experiencing rejections are school and family environments and emotional regulations.

Negative Reactivity and Shyness are Usually Classified as Difficult Temperament

Several researchers examined the moderating role of first-grade classroom quality may have "on the relations between children's difficult temperament (assessed in infancy) and their academic and social outcomes in early elementary school (first grade)" (Curby et al. 2011, 175). A central determinant of classroom quality is the teacher-student interactions. The quality of the interactions that students experienced in the classroom was measured on three domains: emotional support, classroom organization and instructional support. Emotional support refers to teachers' skills to develop a positive classroom environment, meet the children's individual needs and promote responsibility and choices. Classroom organization refers to the teachers having good classroom management skills; behavioural problems do not interfere with learning. In such classrooms, "there is always something for students to work on, and there are variety of ways for students to engage with the materials" (177). Instructional support refers to the teachers' competence "to promote deep thinking about concepts and provide constructive feedback that helps students further engage in the material" (177). Curby et al. (2011) revealed that a quality classroom environment using the abovementioned domains could provide a protective shield against the negative effects of having a difficult temperament. Their data confirmed that classroom interactions, especially emotional support, may be particularly important to children in grade one. Apart from the fact that children are still in their formative years (0–8), they are also transitioning kindergarten to primary, from a high degree of dependency to an environment where there is a greater need to be independent in their learning. Emotionally supportive teachers provide a better fit for children with difficult temperaments. Concerning instructional support, this domain was not affected by the children's temperament; as Curby et al. pointed out, "children with easy temperament and difficult temperaments score similarly" (184). The researchers expanded by stating, "however, in classrooms with lower levels of instructional support, children with more difficult temperaments had less closeness and more conflict with teachers than their peers with easier temperaments" (185). In addition, the researchers reported that organizational support did not seem to differ for children of varying levels of difficult temperament. Again, they expanded: "There was a main effect when looking at grades based on the Mock Report Card, whereby children in more organised classrooms were reported as having higher grades. The present study, therefore, suggests that efforts to improve classroom organization may be beneficial for academics regardless of children's temperament" (185).

It is clear from Curby et al.'s study that children with difficult temperaments need emotional support from their teachers (negative reactivity and shyness). Such support provides a nurturing environment with fewer stress levels, allowing children with negative reactivity and shyness to develop better self-regulatory competence.

Activity Level

Activity level is determined by "the energy level and physical vigour of the child. Children who receive high scores on this scale often run rather than walk, like to play outside, like to participate in sports, and generally are engaged in high levels of gross motor movement" (Martin, Lease and Slobodskya 2020, 15). Children with temperaments that are high in activity level are reflected in mobility during such activities as eating, bathing, playing and dressing. Parents are likely to voice statements such, "I can't leave him on the bed or couch because he always wriggles off"; "he kicks and splashes so in the bath that I always have to mop up the floor afterwards"; "dressing him is a battle he squirms so"; and "he runs around so, that whenever we come in front of the park, I'm exhausted" (Thomas et al. 1964, 44). Hence children with high activity levels are jumping up and down. However, McClowry (2014) noted that their motor activity tends to lessen as children get older. Consequently, when assessing children's activity levels, researchers should always take age into account. In addition to age, Rudasill, Gallagher and White (2010) also suggest that context is an important factor to consider in assessing children's activity level. They explained:

> Depending on the context, high activity level may be viewed as positive or engaged behavior, such as showing enthusiasm (e.g., jumping up and down in excitement about a present), being energetic (e.g., enjoying physical, rather than sedentary, activity), or being inquisitive. In other contexts, and to greater extremes (i.e., very high levels of activity), the temperamental activity dimension may be viewed as negative, or disregulated behavior, such as being overly excited or unable to sit still. Therefore, context and perspective are important when considering whether high activity is positive or negative. High activity levels in home or playground settings may be viewed positively, but high activity in the classroom may be viewed as disruptive. (115)

Children with high activity levels tend to have low attention levels; several authors discuss this association (Rudasill, Gallagher and White 2010; Martin, Lease and Slobodskya 2020). Rudasill, Gallagher, and White's (2010) findings revealed a positive relationship between grade 3 students' achievement and their temperamental assessment at four and a half years of age. They found temperamental attention and activity and classroom emotional support were associated with their mathematics and reading achievement. The results from their study indicated that high emotionally supportive classrooms moderated the relationship between attention and reading and mathematics achievement. Hence poor attention is associated with poor academic performance. When it came to activity level, Rudasill, Gallagher and White's findings showed that children with temperamentally high activity were not poor in their academic achievement. In fact, they found that children who were low in activity, achievement levels were low; while children who were temperamentally high in activity, achievement levels were high. Rudasill, Gallagher and White acknowledged that their results did not align with the results of earlier studies (Palisin 1986; Martin and Holbrook 1985). For example, Palisin findings agreed with Rudasill et al. that good attention span is related to high achievement and that the attention span may influence the relationship between activity and achievement. However, Palisin concluded that the relationship between temperamental activity and students' achievement is unstable because the attributes of activity may include "frenetic play" and "inability to delay", which may reflect impulsivity rather than motor activity. Palisin explained,

> the motorically active child is not necessarily impulsive, and the impulsive child may not be highly active. Nor does it follow that a child who is active will not be able to attend to intellectual tasks (Weithorn, Kagen and Marcus 1984). One can think of children who will engage in gross motor play with abandon, then turn to a more sedentary pursuit such as reading with equal enthusiasm and concentration. (769)

On the other hand, Rudasill, Gallagher and White's findings were more conclusive; they found that children with higher activity levels produced better achievement levels than students with lower activity levels.

It is important to note that high activity levels of children younger than grade three may be seen positively (activities maybe energy, curiosity and motivation). In contrast, older children's activity may be perceived negatively, as the inability to sit still. Rudasill, Gallagher and White's study had a limitation whereby the activity level of the children involved was assessed starting from age four-and-a-half, while their academic achievement was evaluated when these same children were in third grade.

Rudasill, Gallagher and White expanded:

> Activity level prior to the start of formal schooling may be associated with different traits (e.g., energy, curiosity, and motivation) than when measured concurrently with achievement outcomes in school. In the latter case, high activity may be indicative of low inhibitory control or poor behavior regulation (i.e., the inability to sit still). On the other hand, high activity in preschool, or in infancy as found with DiLalla et al. (1990) and Molfese et al. (in press), may be indicative of a willingness to explore and interact with the environment, contributing to a cognitive advantage. (129)

Several authors (McClowry 2014; Martin, Lease and Slobodskya 2020) agree that children with high motor activity levels have difficulty sitting still because of their short attention span. Therefore, such children should be encouraged to engage in sports and other kinesthetic activities.

Task Persistence

Task persistence requires sustained attention and "resistance to the impulse to flee" (Martin, Ryan and Brooks-Gunn 2013). Children with a task persistence temperament start and complete a task; not only are these children able to complete the task, but they are able to maintain engagement with the task. Task persistence involves self-regulation and autonomous behaviours (Martin, Ryan and Brooks-Gunn 2013; McClowry, Hegruk and Teglase 1993; Rothbart and Bates 2006). Self-regulation is characterized by the capacity to control attention, behaviour and emotions (Martin, Ryan and Brooks-Gunn 2013). In other words, children with such temperamental profiles have taken responsibility for their actions and are aware that they can influence the consequences of their actions. In other words, they exhibit autonomous behaviours and are self-directed in accomplishing responsibilities (McClowry, Hegruk and Teglase 1993).

Mokrova et al. (2013) conducted a longitudinal study that examined the role of persistence in the formation of language and mathematical skills (academic skills). Two hundred and sixty-three children at the age of three, persistence and early cognitive-linguistic skills were measured; two years later, their academic skills were assessed. The findings from the study revealed that children as early as the age of three who were more persistent in completing difficult tasks showed greater language and mathematical skills at kindergarten than children who were less persistent in completing challenging tasks. The study implies that children who are low in task persistence will need more assistance from parents and teachers in extending their attention span, especially with challenging tasks. McClowry and Collins (2012) suggested that this could be carried out by dividing these problematic tasks into small components and providing positive acknowledgement when each portion of the task is completed. Children with task persistence temperament are at an advantage because they align with most teachers' expectations of their students, they sit quietly, listen attentively and finished their assigned task. Teachers felt that these students were not only teachable but exhibited high regulatory behaviours in the classroom. Teachers were observed having more positive interactions with these students than with children who were perceived as having more difficult temperaments (McClowry et al. 2013; McClowry 2014).

Approach/Sociability

Students who are high in sociability enjoys the company of others; they are welcoming and warm to unfamiliar persons (Martin, Lease and Slobodskya 2020). In addition, these children demonstrate the need to share in activities with others (Mervielde and De Pauw 2012). They are "expressive, high-spirited, lively, socially potent, physically active and energetic. In contrast, introverted youths are quiet, inhibited and lethargic" (Rothbart and Bates 2006, 311). Thus, sociability may not be evident in children at a very young age. However, as children mature and have more opportunities to interact with peers from diverse backgrounds, sociability temperament becomes more apparent (Zuckerman 2012).

Sociable children are generally excited about school because it is a place to meet and interact with new friends (McClowry 2014). They are always eager to try out new things. They are initiators of interactions. These children are the ones who are likely to reach out to newcomers and show them around the settings and care about these newcomers being social adjusted to the new settings (McClowry 2014). Sociable children exhibit high social competencies; social competence is the capacity to initiate and maintain positive communication. They are able to share, cooperate and collaborate with others (Pekdogan and Kanak 2016). Social competence does not vary from one context to the other. Children who are sociable in temperament tend to be sociable in a variety of contexts. Their social competencies usually result in more positive relationships than shy and withdrawn children. Sendil (2015) study showed that children with high social competencies experienced more positive interactions. Similar to McClowry et al. (2013), Sendil results did not suggest that children differentiated on sociability temperament profile. Sendil explained: "Results of this study revealed that, children with higher peer preference showed more social competence. Moreover, children with higher persistence and approach as temperamental characteristics revealed higher social competence while children with higher reactivity as a temperamental characteristic had also higher anger-aggression behavioral problems. However, gender of children did not differentiate children's social competence, anger-aggression and anxiety withdrawal related behaviors" (V).

Teachers who provide emotional support in the classroom provide a positive, warm, non-threatening and sensitive climate for their children. Children's positive interactions with their teachers predict their success academically. Conversely, children who receive low emotional support are temperamentally at risk for inattentiveness and disruptive behaviour. They are more vulnerable to being counterproductive at school than students with temperamental challenges in a more emotionally supportive classroom.

Jamaican Teachers' Assessment of Students' Temperamental Profiles

A survey was conducted in six primary schools and five basic schools located in Jamaica's urban and rural areas. The sample consisted of five-year-olds and grade 1 students in selected primary and infant schools. Eleven teachers were given specific guidelines to use the instrument to describe their students' behaviour reported on 110 students. These teachers taught the students for at least ten months of one academic year. The data were collected towards the end of the academic year. Teachers were told that the items are not about a child's one-off response to a situation of stress or change but a consistent behaviour style that the child exhibits typically across several situations and settings – these situations could involve stress or change; across context could be in the classroom or on the playfield; the keyword was *consistency*.

Procedure for Selecting the Sample

Each teacher was responsible for doing temperament profiles on ten children (five boys and five girls). First, the ten students were selected using the raffle or lottery-type of sampling. Then, the names of the students were given to the research assistants. There were two research assistants in each classroom. They separated the names of the boys in one bag and the names of the girls in another bag. After shaking up the bags with the names – five boys and five girls were selected for the teacher to produce temperament profiles.

Teacher School Age Temperament (T-SATI)

Temperament was primarily measured using standardized rating scales that were rated by a teacher describing each child in classroom behaviour. T-SATI (Teacher School-Age Temperament Inventory), developed by Sandee McClowry, New York University, allows teachers to describe their students' behaviour. For example,

1. Is shy with adults he or she doesn't know.
2. Gets upset when there is a change in plans.
3. Remembers to do assignments without being reminded.
4. Quits routine classroom assignments before finished.

It should be noted that the methods used to determine children's and adults' temperaments are different. Instruments concerning children's temperaments are rated by the parents, teachers or peers, while for adults, temperament measure is self-rated.

Results and Discussion

Similar to Cook and Lipps (2020), the teachers who participated in this present study scored the students highest on task persistence (M=3.50; SD=.0.08), with the small standard deviation suggesting an agreement among the eleven teachers; while the lowest score was negative reactivity (M=2.55; SD=0.31) (See table 5.1).

Table 5.1: Means, SDs, and Cronbach's Alpha of the T-SATI Dimensions

	N	Mean	Std. Deviation	α
Task Persistence	109	3.50	0.08	0.86
Withdrawal	110	2.58	0.44	0.77
Negative Reactivity	110	2.55	0.31	0.89
Activity	110	2.73	0.31	0.88
Valid N (listwise)	109			

According to Cook and Lipps (2020), participating teachers, in a similar group of Jamaican teachers scored their students the highest on task persistence (M=3.10; SD=0.41) and negative reactivity the lowest score (M=2.60, SD=0.63).

Activity was given the second-highest score in both studies; in this present study, Activity was scored M=2.73 with a standard deviation of 0.31. Cook and Lipps reported M=2.88, with a standard deviation of 2.88, SD=0.43).

The high score on task persistence for children ages five and six years suggest that children in the early childhood classroom are more likely to sit and complete tasks. Similar findings were revealed in the Mokrova et al. (2013) study; they reported that children as young as three years old were task persistent in completing a challenging task. In addition, these children showed higher achievement in language and maths than their peers who had lower task persistence scores. McClowry and Collins (2012) reported that the students who scored high in task persistence also scored low on negative reactivity and activity and therefore were less likely to require as much teachers' attention as their peers. Teachers must plan for both groups of students in distinct ways. Understanding children's temperament will clarify the reasons and methods by which children vary in their behaviours, actions and reactions, thereby enhancing their academic experiences (McCorwick 2014; Bakken, Brown and Downing 2017). Teachers at the early childhood level must understand that early childhood education does have a long-term impact on students' future experience at school.

Summary

In this chapter, a more expanded discussion of the core attributes of temperament, reactivity and self-regulation was given. Four types of temperament (negative reactivity, shyness, task persistence, activity and sociableness) linked to the core attributes were discussed in more detail to understand children's temperamental differences better. The chapter culminates in presenting and discussing an empirical study involving 110 five-year-old students and eleven teachers. The teachers were asked to describe each student's temperament by responding to the T-SATI instrument developed by Sandee McClowry to identify a student's temperamental profile. The results show that teacher responses indicate that students with task persistence profiles seemed to dominate their classrooms.

6. INSIGHTS into Children's Temperament Programme

In 2011, as a visiting Fulbright scholar at New York University, the author was introduced to Professor Sandee McClowry, developer of the INSIGHTS programme. This introduction stirred my interest in bringing the programme to Jamaica for the following reasons:

- I had not heard of a programme in Jamaica that helps teachers and parents to understand differences in children's characteristics.
- I did not know of a programme that was comprehensive in one setting. For the ten-week sessions, parents, teachers and children in any one week were being taught the principles of the programme, and most of the principles were common to the three groups: this facilitated interactions and a sense of working towards a common goal among the participants.
- I liked the fact that conflicts and problems in relationships were seen as a dilemma, which suggests that there is always a solution. Instead of being permanently offended, individuals can work to resolve problems. The offender is not considered better than the person being offended, and vice versa; both parties have a problem. The programme

empowers the offender and gives him/her tools from an early age to resolve conflicts and bullying.

- I also liked the lessons learned from the programme. Children learn to not expect others to be like them. They eventually realize that each of their peers has a different temperament; they are all unique. In the children's sessions, they sing the following song at the beginning and the end:

> I'm unique (clap, clap). You're unique (clap, clap). We're all unique (clap, clap). And that's just fine. I'm unique (clap, clap). You're unique (clap, clap). We're all unique (clap, clap). And that's just fine (What?) And that's just fine.

- From very early, children learn that it is alright for others to be different; and so they celebrate rather than scorn differences.

- The programme is very interactive and allows participants, to an extent, to reflect and share their experiences

I discussed the details of the INSIGHTS programme with Dr Rose Davies, the then leading expert in Early Childhood Education in the Caribbean. Dr Davies was in full support of importing the programme to the Jamaican context. However, before doing so, a team of educator including Dr Rose Davies, Dr Marcia Stewart, Mrs Winsome Johns Gayle from the Early Childhood Commission (ECC), Prof. Zelleynne Jennings Craig (then director of the School of Education) and myself decided to pilot the programme with a group of teacher educators and get their views on the relevance of the programme to Jamaica's early childhood context. Based on this decision, Prof. McClowry and her husband, Dr Mark Spellman, came to Jamaica to supervise the piloting of the INSIGHTS programme.

As a preliminary phase in the pilot in 2012, a three-day workshop was carried out with Jamaican teacher trainers, development officers and persons in supervisory positions from the ECC. These participants were very positive about the principles of the INSIGHTS intervention and felt that the content of the programme was very relevant to the Jamaican context. McClowry and Spellman (2016) reported that these attendees thought that the INSIGHTS programme would provide practical strategies for parenting and classroom management. They indicated that educators voiced the following:

- Many of our parents and teachers are throwing up their arms in despair as they have run out of options to control their children. Teachers have given up on some students as they are unable to pay attention to lessons. INSIGHTS provides options that are likely to work in Jamaican homes and schools.
- INSIGHTS will help teachers work with children instead of being aggressive (beating).
- It gives alternatives and options.
- Quite a number of teachers, parents and caregivers do not know how to deal with our children ... we do place great emphasis on beating and hitting to discipline ... it would be most relevant to try something new that has been proving to work. (84)

McClowry and Spellman (2016) also reported the effect of the workshop on the participants. The teacher educators had this to say:

> I, for one, was linking the students' temperament (Gregory the Grumpy) with being rude or disrespectful. But I was enlightened to know that it's not being rude or out of order, but it's just their personality, and we have to help them to self-monitor until they can manage themselves. The situation is two-way – the students need to understand their temperament and, as educators, we need to understand how children think and behave so as not to abuse or mislabel them as misfits.
>
> I have developed tolerance for the pouting, sulky child, and practiced ways to help him/her to share the way he/she

feels. Previously, my comments were to jolt the child out of his/her sullenness, assuming that his actions or inactions mocked my authority. Now, I embrace and acknowledge his/her expressions as both good and bad signs of how he/she feels and, as such, can now conduct my actions/reaction accordingly and favourably. (86)

The INSIGHTS programme targets early childhood, which is the most sensitive period of brain and character development. The programme also targets teachers and parents and children in under-resourced communities. The developer of INSIGHTS is aware of the influence of the environment on students' character development and ultimately, their behaviour. So INSIGHTS programme challenges parents and teachers to be sensitive in creating an environment conducive the healthy development of emotionally stable individuals.

It is imperative whenever an intervention is implemented that an assessment is done. Such an assessment will help the programme manager to be attuned with the extent to which participants have benefited from the intervention. As a result, the last three chapters focused on an assessment of the impact of the intervention.

The School of Education (UWI) received funding from the CHASE Fund, Jamaica, for the INSIGHTS in Jamaica Programme for three years (2014–17) to support the intervention in urban areas. Within this period, the School of Education also received funds for one academic year (2014–15) from the Alumni Engagement Innovation Fund through the Embassy of the United States of America; this fund was used to expand the INSIGHTS project into several rural early childhood institutions. As a result, between January 2014 and August 2016, the INSIGHTS project reached early child institutions in urban schools in the Kingston metropolitan, focusing on institutions in under-resourced communities four rural institutions. The participants from these institutions totalled 3,560 children, 193 parents and 112 teachers.

The Operational Structure of INSIGHTS in Jamaica

The INSIGHTS intervention in Jamaica has three phases – initiation, re-entry and licensing:

- The initiation phase: This phase occurs in the first semester when the school receives the programme. The facilitators are the Development Officers from ECC and INSIGHTS team.
- The re-entry phase: At the end of the initiation period, the schools are invited to re-enter the programme. The School of Education sponsored the training of school-based facilitators by providing venues and lunch forms. Schools that re-enter are responsible for selecting a suitable candidate (a senior teacher or guidance counsellor) who would be responsible for timetabling the sessions and implementing the programme in their schools. This phase gives the schools an opportunity to evaluate their capability and interest in continuing the programme in their schools for licensing. It also allows the coordinators of the INSIGHTS Jamaica programme to assess the schools' capacity to implement the teachers' and children's sessions of the programme into the school's schedule of activities.
- Licensed phase: A licensed school is an institution that has received initial implementation of the intervention and has successfully completed the re-entry period of the intervention. At this point, the school-based facilitator has complete responsibility to implement the programme, and he or she is monitored periodically by the INSIGHTS team to ensure fidelity. Also, the school pays the INSIGHTS programme organizers a licensing fee for rental of the INSIGHTS toolkit. The licence is renewed at the beginning of each academic year.

The three phases of INSIGHTS were originally structured by Jamaica to assist with the sustainability of the programme in the schools. By adding a school-based component into the INSIGHTS programme, schools can embed its INSIGHTS principles into their culture, leading to improved behaviour management by both teachers in school and parents at home, as well as fostering better interactions among students. This reduces aggression and conflict in the schools and equips young students with the necessary skills to manage their own responses to the various dilemmas that present themselves not only in their academic situation but also in their everyday life as they grow and mature into the next generation of adults.

At the start of each academic year, the ECC identifies six basic and infant schools for participation in the INSIGHTS intervention per academic year. In the first year of the implementation of INSIGHTS, the ECC allowed three development officers (DCs) from the Commission to work along with the INSIGHTS team to implement the programme in the selected schools. From semester two of the academic year 2013–14 to semester one of the academic year 2014–15, the facilitators of the programme were Commission DCs. For the above-mentioned period, the DCs facilitated the sessions for the three groups of participants: ten half-hour sessions once per week for children; and ten two-hour sessions on separate days for parents and teachers. However, in semester two of the academic year 2014–15, two members of the INSIGHTS team became responsible for the parent's sessions – the programme manager and the coordinator. As time progressed, the parents' sessions and teachers' sessions had to be reduced to six and eight weeks, respectively. The hours were reduced because both groups complained that a two-hour session for ten weeks was too long and demanding.

INSIGHTS is a promising, temperament-based intervention for helping parents and teachers to understand the children they are responsible for and to be more thoughtful when disciplining them. Parents and teachers are given a framework to use as a guide to assess their own thinking about behavioural management strategies, and to implement these strategies for the benefit of the child, thus minimizing their frustration. Children are equipped, from an early age, with conflict management strategies that will allow them to be less frustrated and less aggressive as they develop.

Assessment of the INSIGHTS Programme

After two years of implementation in Jamaica (2014–16), nineteen schools participated in the intervention (fifteen urban schools and four rural schools). A total of 3,036 children, 169 parents and 88 teachers from urban and rural communities have received the INSIGHTS programme. All of the urban schools were public schools located mostly in under-resourced communities. This study is mainly qualitative. However, the quantitative data are presented to give the audience an example of how parents and teachers quantitatively rated the usefulness of the INSIGHTS principles about behavioural management. Both quantitative and qualitative feedback were only obtained from parents and teachers. In 2021, the INSIGHTS team also collected qualitative data using two focus groups from teachers who work at a school that participated in INSIGHTS from the initial implementation in Jamaica in 2013. Since the end of the CHASE funds, we have continued to support schools that received the intervention during the three years we received funding. We report on this data in the final chapter.

The data for the quantitative results were gathered from approximately twelve parents over ten weeks from four schools (in total, forty-eight parents participated); three schools within the urban areas and one school in a rural community. A total of 123 evaluation sheets were collected from parents at the end of the programme. Also, data were gathered from eleven teachers over ten weeks from three schools in the urban areas and one school in a rural community. A total of seventy-one evaluation sheets were collected from teachers at the end of the programme.

The focus group discussions, which were carried out at the end of each week of the intervention for 2014–16, collected qualitative data. Each school had two focus groups on location, one for teachers and the other for parents. A semi-structured interview protocol was used by research assistants to guide the focus group discussions. Each focus group was assigned two research assistants, a moderator and a scribe. Approximately 169 parents and 88 teachers from urban and rural communities participated in the focus group discussions.

The four transcripts from the focus group interviews were coded manually initially, using the conventional content analysis technique. Therefore, the coding categories were derived from the content of the transcripts (Lichtman 2013). Final coding was done with the aid of QDA Miner, a qualitative data analysis software. The results are reported on in the next two chapters.

Summary

In this chapter, the INSIGHTS into Children's Temperament intervention is described, and evidence of programme effectiveness presented. With temperament theory as its framework, INSIGHTS provides parents and teachers with a structure for appreciating the individual differences of children. The programme helps parents and teachers with replacing harsh disciplinary strategies with responsive ones that more align with the child's temperament. Parents and teachers are challenged to consider having a differentiated approach to their behaviour management of children.

Though the teacher sessions are held separately from parents' sessions, the content of the curriculum is very similar. They are introduced to ways in which temperament influences a child's behaviour and emotional reactions. The positives and challenges of each temperament (friendly, grumpy, cautious and hardworking) are discussed. The adults are exposed to the difference between creating a goodness of fit and a poorness of fit environment. All ten sessions are described concisely. A brief description of the children's sessions is included. The reprise song "I'm Unique. You're Unique" reflects that the core principle of these sessions is accepting self and others. Students learn from very early to accept that in our everyday life, there are always dilemmas to be solved. They are equipped with problem-solving skills and strategies.

At the close of this chapter, the reader is presented with research evidence concerning the effectiveness of INSIGHTS. INSIGHTS assisted teachers in improving the goodness-of-fit between a child's temperament and the academic learning context. The intervention was found to increase the academic achievement; sustained students' attention and reduced disruptive behaviour problems of first-grade children.

7. The Influence of INSIGHTS on Parenting Practice

Parenting can promote or hamper children's development as healthy adults (Reebye 2005; Sullivan-Schoppe et al. 2008; Kline Pruett, Arthur and Ebling 2007; Bertoni et al. 2017). To be an effective parent who promotes healthy development in a child is not without challenges. Becoming parents, especially when parenting is suddenly tossed on them, is even more challenging. Parents have varying abilities, styles and backgrounds (Bertoni et al. 2017). Often, parents are not sure of their responsibilities; they struggle with what this role should be. There are several parenting interventions, such as the Bertoni et al.'s (2017) intervention – Groups for Family Enrichment – targeted helping parents through reflection to address the following questions:

- Who am I as a parent?
- What are parents' responsibilities and the characteristics of the parenting role?
- What is the ideal parent like?
- What kind of parent am I compared to other parents I know?

Bertoni et al. concluded that their intervention had the following impact:

> The passage from fear to idealization, to legitimation of self and the other, can be a reliable base for a deeper work on parental competencies. Without this enrichment of parental identity, the work on parental skills may remain superficial and dissolve in the long run. (227)

Whereas Groups for Family Enrichment_Parent (GFE_P) focused on parents only during the intervention, INSIGHTS as a comprehensive programme for improving classroom behaviour includes parents, teachers and children. So, while parents are engaged in a ten-week session (two hours per week), the teachers are involved in sessions with a similar duration, and the children are involved in half-hour sessions each week for the same period. This chapter delves into parents' perspectives on the contribution of the INSIGHTS temperament programme to enhancing their approach to behavioural management with their children. It also examines their comments regarding their child-rearing practices prior to participating in the programme. Parents' likes and dislikes regarding the programme are discussed, their suggestions for amendments to the programme and how the programme can be increased into the wider Jamaican society.

What INSIGHTS Revealed about Parents

Parents in the under-resourced communities selected for the INSIGHTS intervention revealed that they had no mental framework for what type of parent they would like to be to their children before actually becoming parents. Parenting seemed to have been approached in a very unstructured, haphazard manner, which makes these parents vulnerable to repeating the mistakes of their own parents.

Parents confessed to administering harsh parenting strategies, such as shouting, corporal punishment, and verbal and emotional abuse. They compared their children with other children, and some parents voiced rejection of their children. As these parents lacked understanding of their children's characters, they resorted to verbal abuse. In addition, they misinterpreted their children's personality constraints for rudeness or deliberate attempts on the part of the child to be defiant to the parent, even at the young age of five. Focus group discussions revealed that beating and shouting, before the INSIGHTS intervention, were the main strategies that parents used when children misbehaved and needed parental guidance. However, there were a few parents who reported exercising good parenting skills in under-resourced communities.

Parents ineffectively administered corporal punishment as they felt that this was an easier strategy to discipline children than to talk to them. The parents voiced:

> We, as inner-city people, we don't take talk, so the least little thing, we beat the pickney dem.

> Before, I was buff baff baff baff and so, but now you have to ... basically it (referring to the programme) just help you with your temper. Because, as parents, the first thing you do is shout.

> Umm, at first, I didn't know much about parenting because everything my son does mi beat him, hard to, my mother use to seh me ago a prison, so, coming here (INSIGHTS) everything changes.

> My experience with the programme was OK, because I get to know certain things, because I use to beat Kayla and I stop beat her now. I use to shout, but am using signal now, so it was very helpful for me and Kayla and also my other siblings at home.

> Hands down, every day I talk, 'Boy mi nuh know weh mi have u fah, mi nuh know wah mek u come suh', or those things. Sometimes, you a talk and some things come to u mind. A suh me behave with my son, cause him give me a lot of trouble. (Participant M)

Additionally, two mothers were recorded as referring to themselves as "bully mothers".

Parenting in Jamaica involve harsh discipline practices, especially among parents in under-resourced communities (Fernald and Meeks-Gardner 2003; Harriott and Jones 2016; Serrbanescu, Ruiz, and Suchdev 2010). For example, Fernald and Meeks-Gardner (2003) noted that children reported that:

> [Mother] Beat, cook, wash, work. (male)
>
> [Father] Beat. Him take the rubbish out the back yard. (female)
>
> [Father] Lick [Hit] you. Thump [Hit] you down. Beat you on your bottom. (female)
>
> [Father] Look after them children. Some of the father beat you sometime. (129)

Fernald and Meeks-Gardner (2003) also concluded that "parents seemed to have a role, not just in administering punishment, but also in educating their children about violence and how to respond to aggression" (129). Both fathers and mothers would encourage their children to retaliate with equal physical aggression if another child should "hit them" (129). Serrbanescu, Ruiz and Suchdev (2010), reported that 61.2 per cent of the women sampled, who were between the ages of fifteen and twenty-four, noted that before the age of fifteen, they were shoved, hit, kicked or slapped by a parent or stepparent. Harriott and Jones (2016) noted that "parenting style also affects children's psychosocial outcomes and contributes to transmission of violence" (28).

Parental frustration seemed to result from the parents' lack of understanding of their children. This lack leads them to view the negative, reactive part of the children's temperament as the purposeful intention of the children to be rude and disrespectful. Parents voiced:

> I didn't know it was temperament. I thought the child was just having bad attitude and the child is bad and all of that. I didn't know it was temperament until INSIGHTS programme started.
>
> For me, I just said that the child didn't have any manners.
>
> Before the programme, mi never look at it and say boy is the child temperament. Mi just think the pickney feisty or rude.

Parents Feedback on the Influence of INSIGHTS Intervention

Overall, it appears, from the parents' quantitative feedback, that INSIGHTS provided helpful information for addressing their children's behavioural problems at home. Ninety-seven per cent of the parents rated the facilitators highly. However, not all parents who participated in the programme could read, so the focus group gave more comprehensive feedback on parents' views on the influence of INSIGHTS on their interactions with their children. Parents would quietly indicate this to the facilitator when handed out the evaluation sheets; also, when there should be reporting of homework activities.

How often did you use what you learnt in INSIGHTS?

Based on the 123 evaluation sheets collected from parents, approximately 81 per cent of the responses suggest parents used the information learnt in INSIGHTS very often (see figure 7.1).

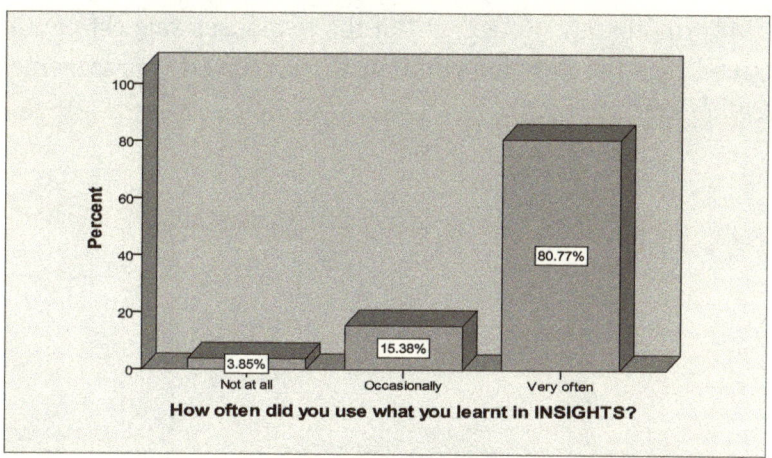

Figure 7.1: How often did parents use what they learnt from INSIGHTS?

How much did you learn?

Approximately 83 per cent of the responses indicated that parents felt they learned *a great deal of new information* (see figure 7.2).

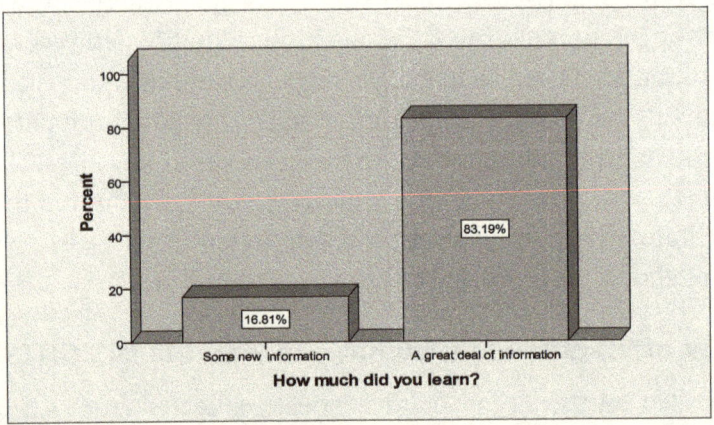

Figure 7.2: How much did parents learn?

How useful was the new information you received?

Approximately 96 per cent of the responses suggest parents agreed that the new information they received was *extremely useful* (see figure 7.3).

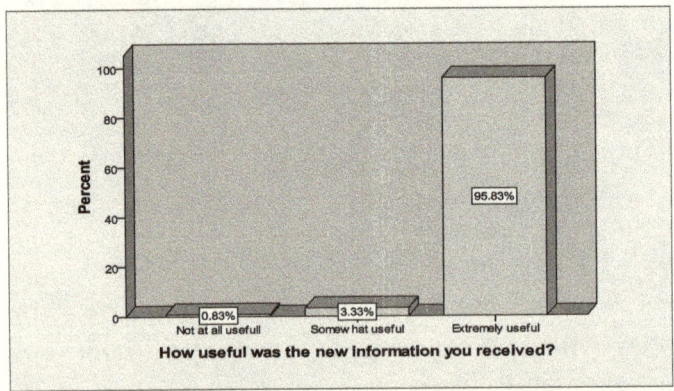

Figure 7.3: How useful did parents find the information received?

How effective was your facilitator?

Approximately 97 per cent of the responses suggest parents rated their facilitators as *highly effective* (see figure 7.4).

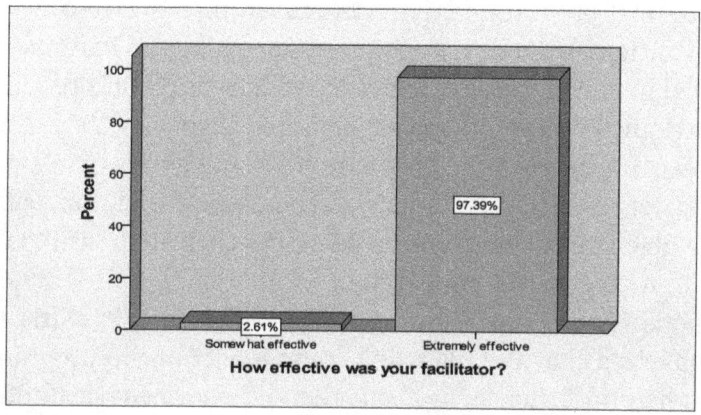

Figure 7.4:   How did the parents rate the facilitators?

What Parents Liked about INSIGHTS

Parents developed new insights into their children's behaviour by understanding the concept of temperament and identifying the different temperament profiles. Self-knowledge or self-awareness for parents is another principle that is purported by the programme. Self-awareness is embedded in the session on Social Competencies for Parents and Categories of Parental Responses.

The programme guided parents in how to foster social competence. Social competence is the skills and behaviour required to manage oneself socially and emotionally to pursue healthy relationships. Parents need to develop these competencies when relating to their children so that their children will, in turn, learn how to establish positive relationships with other adults and their peers (Pekdogan and Kanak 2016). Social competencies include listening, responding, controlling their temper, empathy, etc., rather than reacting to their child. Parents were also encouraged to develop a contract with themselves to improve specific social competency skills. Then, through self-awareness, parents can carry out corrective measures for their behaviours. In the INSIGHTS programme, parents realize that they too need to change their behaviour, not just their children. Parents were guided in how to assess their responses to the child's request or behaviour. For parents to evaluate their response, they need to be aware of themselves. There are three categories of responses – counterproductive, adequate and optimal. In addition, parents were given guidelines on how to assess their response to their children quickly. Parents in their reflection felt that INSIGHTS influenced a change in their perspectives and behaviours. They emphasized that the following components of the programme were helpful – Learning about the Temperament of Children, Guidelines for Self-awareness, and How to Structure Responses with high negative reactivity.

Learning about Temperament

Understanding the different temperaments helped parents to reframe how they viewed their children. They learned to accept their children's uniqueness, celebrate differences and take responsibility for helping their children manage their negative reactions.

Parents must acknowledge that similarities between individuals do not imply sameness and should celebrate the diversity and beauty found in differences. Concerning the acceptance of differences, parents are guided to recognize that discipline strategies are not a one-size-fits-all (INSIGHTS Manual 1999). Each child has to be trained in a different way – different from even how they, as parents, were taught by their own parents. Parents voiced the following:

> Now I know and I learn also that temperament is also another name for personality. I also realize that every child [have] a different temperament and you should not compare your

child. Our childhood was different from now, so we can't treat our child the same way as our parents treat us in the past. So, learn to do away with the past . . .

Now I understand that's how he was born because the temperament was within.

I learn how to manage Jaquan high temperament; he is high in reactivity. I get mad easily when he is up and down, all over the place. But now I get to understand him more better, so he is calm when he is around the place.

First, mi neva really know how fi deal wid when my son a act di way him act. Now mi find out weh Gregory the grumpy mean, and suh, knowing the different temperament, me can label my son and seh him a deh one deh suh. Mi know how fi deal wid him betta now, when me see him a act deh way deh. Now mi jus tink back pan weh mi learn, and seh u know seh a suh mi fi deal wid dah situation yah.

The INSIGHTS temperament styles helped the parents to reframe how they viewed their children's negative reactions. It is important to note that, in the INSIGHTS programme, parents are cautioned not to label their children with temperament profiles. However, temperament profiles are tools for parents to use to compare and contrast their children's temperaments in a quest to understand their children better. So, the temperament profiles enhance understanding and allow parents to see the areas of their children's temperaments that they need to assist their children in managing the negative reactions of their characteristics. The parents' statements during the focus group discussion suggest that, during and after their participation, they were a lot more relaxed and appreciative of their children, and they experienced a feeling of empowerment in dealing with their children's negative reactions:

It take away some of the ignorance, and some of the madness.

I am the parent of a grade one child and prior to coming here, I would have used the term that he is a problem child, but now the term that is used for him is high maintenance.

Effective parenting can serve as a "protective process and enhance the resiliency of children" (McClowry, Snow and Tamis-Lemonda 2005, 568). Parents' caring and positive involvement in the management of their children's behaviour at the early childhood level is more likely to result in children's increased competence in managing their own behaviours. As parents understand their children's temperaments and can respond rather than react to the negative aspect of their children's temperaments, the parents' efficacy to manage their children's behaviour increases. O'Connor et al. (2012) reported that using the instrument, Parental Daily Report (PDR), they measured the extent to which children's behaviour improved following the INSIGHTS intervention. They reported:

> Children with high maintenance temperaments evidenced greater rates of decline in PDR scores than their industrious peers during the course of the intervention, leading to an 8.5-point difference in behavior problems between the two groups at final assessment, compared with a nearly 13-point preintervention gap. The greater decrease in behavior problems for children with high maintenance temperaments might relate to the INSIGHTS curriculum that teaches caregivers strategies to match a child's temperament, particularly challenging ones. (10)

As these children get older, they are less likely to become deviant and aggressive in their behaviour and more likely to exhibit positive behavioural outcomes. When parents manage children's behaviour with warmth and effective discipline strategies, behaviour problems are minimized at the early childhood stage of development.

Self-awareness

The INSIGHTS programme provides a structure for parenting that allows the parents to reflect on who they are as persons, who they are as parents, and who they would like to be in relating to their children. Thus, parents who participate in the programme are equipped with a mental framework of what they would like the parenting of their children to be like. The programme also allows them to become aware that they were underthinking their role as parents, thereby treating their children harshly. It is important to note that aggression is more natural to human beings than the principles of managing aggression. Thus, Tremblay stated that "the studies on the frequency of physical aggression during the early childhood years indicate that children do not need to learn to use physical aggression from their environment; they rather learn not to use physical aggression" (Tremblay 2012, 2).

In the INSIGHTS programme, parents learn to take responsibility for their actions. For example, several of the parents confessed that they shouted when correcting their child. When correcting children, parents learn during the INSIGHTS sessions to not focus only on their children's actions but to be self-aware when correcting or disciplining their children. Children may be similar or different from their parents. Sometimes the similarities can cause issues between parents and children, or sometimes differences cause issues. Parents are therefore invited to reflect on their personality and assess the extent of their negative reactivity during the programme. The facilitators are trained to guide parents in becoming more self-aware. The programme seemed to have enhanced parents' self-awareness about their parental skills and behaviour through the Social Competences and Parental Responses sessions. Participants, reflecting on the impact of the programme, voiced the following:

> I was very frustrated. I think the programme has helped first with self-esteem. So knowing yourselves and understanding yourselves, it helps you to feel better. Then understanding the child makes a bigger impact both mentally and socially.

> This is the best that could ever happen to me. It helps me to deal with my temper toward my child. Thank you so much.

> It help us to deal with ourselves because we ignorant and all of that.

Based on the temperament and myself in terms of understanding, I feel good. The reason why I feel good is because I understand what it is to deal with the different temperament that the child has now. I know, it wouldn't be easy though, but now I can control myself on a level because I never had that control. I am very snappy; the least little thing, I just snap. But now, I have an idea. I can now take a breather and now try to deal with that kinda temperament that I have, now knowing the child's needs as a parent.

Parents Response Categories: Self-evaluation

There were three categories of responses that parents were exposed to in the programme: counterproductive, adequate and optimal. Parents use these categories to assess their response to children's behaviours and requests (Graham McClowry 2003):

- **Counterproductive**: This is a parental response that only makes the situation worse Counterproductive responses are usually expressed in an angry tone and involve shouting and saying negative words.
- **Adequate:** This is a parental response that is expected to resolve the situation quickly and is spoken in more of a neutral manner.
- **Optimal:** This parental response is intended to help the child to develop and mature. "It acknowledges the individuality of the child by remarking about his or her temperament or desires. Optimal statements are relayed in a warm and understanding manner" (30). Optimal responses challenge the child's competency to problem solve. So instead of the parent suggesting possible solutions to the child's problem, the parents ask questions that guide the child in finding solutions for his or her problems.

In the programme, parents are trained to monitor themselves and their reactions as they discipline their children. Parents gave the following feedback:

I like the optimal and adequate strategies because it helps me not to be counterproductive. For the optimal, you don't shout, you speak in a calm way. Adequate (let me go back to my book). You resolve the situation quickly; speak softly to the person in a neutral way. Both are good. Both are used to resolve situations.

I now know how to deal with my peers, not only my children.

I am happy I was a part of the programme; the session opened my eyes to different ways of dealing with situations. Now I will not be counterproductive, then feel bad afterwards. Have grown as a parent, listening more. Accomplished, in that I am now able to deal with other children, other than my child, and now minimize the "good and bad" comparison among different children.

Parents liked the programme because the principles were practical. They viewed video vignettes that dramatized each behaviour style. Parents were able to implement the principles in their own lives and experienced changes in their perceptions of their children and their role as parents. The principles learned in the programme were also extended beyond their children; they applied the principles to their children's friends and children in their communities.

Change in Parental Use of Competencies in Response to Children

Through the social competencies' sessions, parents improved their competence in two-way communication with their children. An improvement in parents' social competencies meant a decrease in harsh and aggressive responses from parents to their children. Participating parents emphasized the need for social competencies (such as listening). Parents were stimulated to seek to understand their children and develop an attitude of responding rather than reacting to their negative actions. Parents were given guidelines on how to be a better listener, for example by:

- Paying attention to what the other person is telling you
- Letting the other person know that you understand by saying, for example:
- "That must have been difficult for you."
- "I understand why you are frustrated."
- Asking questions when you do not understand, etc. (INSIGHTS Manual 1999, 50).

Several parents reported listening more to their children and shouted less. By listening, they gained a better understanding of their children's character and actions. Parents voiced the following:

> I listen more before I react.

> INSIGHTS helped me to listen to my children more, "stopped eating the message".

> The programme very good; I don't have to shout at her. I talk to her and she sit and listen (note that the parent said the child sit and listen – keep in mind that this child is also involved in the INSIGHTS programme)

Parents were guided in developing contracts with their children concerning behaviour that they felt "stuck", that is, repetitious and annoying behaviour. Parents were trained in the sessions to involve their child "in selecting the goal, the child/parent responsibilities and the reinforcements" (INSIGHTS Manual 1999, 36). These contracts were meant to achieve mutual benefits between parent and child. INSIGHTS also guided parents and teachers on using a contract to work on a selected area that teachers would like parents to assist the child with at home. Parents expressed these views about the agreement:

> The contract, because when they are doing something, like you confuse, and you tell them that, umm if you don't do that then you are going to get a sticker, and you have the stickers and show them the stickers and they pick the one that they want and you say to them that if you don't behave yourself

then you are not going to get the sticker, and it works because my son get the stickers and he behave his self.

The contract, because my daughter, when she wakes up in the morning, she gives a lot of trouble. Like she nuh ready fi bathe yet, and she nuh ready, suh because my son does not know now who take her to school in the morning, so him always a seh 'deh little girl yah a mek mi late enuh'. Suh me seh mek me comb har hair like one fi the week and a morning time now you get up and you nuh bada gi nuh problem and she just come sidung wid di comb and every week now she just start comb her hair and she get her sticker, suh she nuh give me any problem.

Changes Parents Observed in Their Children

Though INSIGHTS involve parents, teachers and children simultaneously, the programme's goal is to minimize children's disruptive and aggressive behaviours. Several parents reported that they observed changes in their children's behaviour at home. For example, Parent 1 below expressed that she observed changes both in the child's behaviour and her behaviour as a parent. This parent used "time-out", another strategy taught in the programme. For Parent 2 (see below), the change was observed in the child's academic performance:

Parent 1: My son, he was very intolerable, and since he is coming to the programme that I am coming, and my mom and dad they couldn't tek it, and now since he is coming, him change, because they use different procedures, and I saw change. His behaviour change. He use to answer back, and him nuh duh that gain. Him shake up himself. Him nah duh that again. When he use to [misbehave], me beat him, but now mi tell him fi go sidung – time out.

Parent 2: This programme is a good programme, and I think the contract was the best idea for my child. Also, she has improved a lot in her writing skills and learning. Thanks to INSIGHTS.

Parents' Views on the Demands of INSIGHTS

During the focus group discussions, parents were asked to give their views on the constraints of the programme. Parents indicated three major constraints: remembering the different tasks, doing homework and implementing the strategies. Several parents had challenges reading and felt that too much emphasis was placed on written reporting of the home activities.

Training Strategies Most Liked by Parents

Parents enjoyed watching the videos and doing role play during their training sessions. Video-taped vignettes of mini-dramas with professional actors provided a window into parent-child interactions. The vignettes allowed the viewers to see and experience the various strategies recommended by INSIGHTS, including those counter-productive strategies. The videos also facilitated interactive discussions. For example, one parent voiced the following concerning the videos:

> Yea, what we all basically do is that we inject our live experiences, and the videos inject live experiences, so we get to understand more.

The Puppet That Parents Likened Their Child to the Most or the Least

At the beginning of the programme, parents were encouraged to select one of their children (if they had more than one) to work within the programme. Most parents associated their "problem child" with Gregory the Grumpy. Gregory is regarded as high maintenance; he reacts strongly and negatively to changes or stressful situations. He gets upset quickly and can be very moody.

A positive side to high maintenance children is that they are often comfortable making decisions and expressing their opinions, even when others disagree. Parents who attended the programme were told that they make good leaders. Data revealed that most parents associated the child they selected to work on in the programme with Gregory. The least selected were Coretta (shy and withdrawn) and Fredrico (the friendly). The narrative shows that parents did not align Hillary with the child they needed to help but just mentioned that they have Hillary, the hard worker, and Gregory, the grumpy.

Parents' Descriptions of the INSIGHTS Programme

Parents were asked to select one word that best describes their experience of the INSIGHTS programme (see figure 7.11).

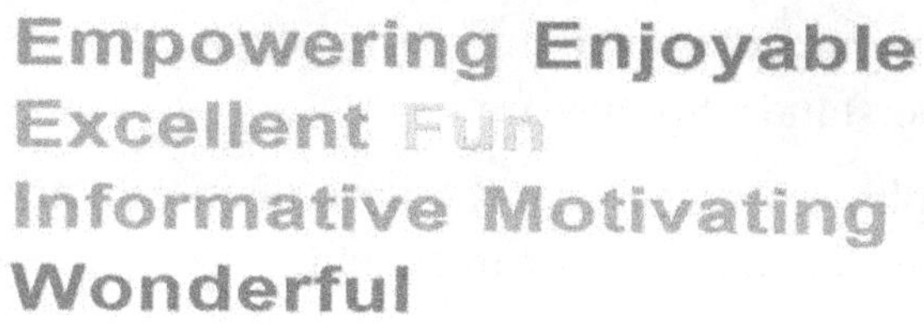

Empowering Enjoyable
Excellent Fun
Informative Motivating
Wonderful

Figure 7.5: Parents Words That Describe How They Found the INSIGHTS Experience

The quantitative results (see figures 7.2–7.4), which reflected parents' positive attitudes towards the programme, were explained in more detail by the qualitative findings. For example, figure 7.4 shows that 96 per cent of the responses suggest that parents found the new information *very useful*. From the qualitative, we learned that the INSIGHTS programme changed parents' perspectives on temperament, self-awareness and how to structure their response to children's problem behaviours. Overall, parents felt very positive about the programme and some even voiced that the programme ended too quickly, see the following exemplary comment.

> I learnt a lot, and I just learnt how to ignore her [the child] because that is one of the things I have to do. I learn how to ignore her when she is crying, I just walk away, take time out, as we learn in the programme. So, I am not ready for the

programme to end. I was learning so much, and I think they are so much more to learn from this programme.

Parents' Recommendation for the INSIGHTS Programme

The parents recommended the following for the programme:
- The programme should be aired on local television (via commercials) and should be a part of the curriculum in all teachers' colleges.
- The parenting programmes should begin from an early childhood level. If parents understand their children's temperaments from an early stage, they will better understand who they are.
- Display information in the form of an exhibition so that the wider community can benefit.
- Produce a radio talk show that would allow participants in the INSIGHTS programme to pass on the information they learnt to the wider community.
- The scenes in the video productions should be more Jamaicanized; they are too Americanized.

Parents considered learning about different temperaments and being guided in the principles of self-awareness and the principles of optimal, adequate and counterproductive responses to be of equal value for enhancing their competencies as parents. Focusing on children's temperaments helped the parents to better appreciate their role as parents. INSIGHTS challenged parents to take note of their responsibility in nurturing their children's emotional development. Instead of taking this emotional development for granted, the parents now understand the extent to which they can cause their children emotional stress as children are not fully developed in their self-awareness and self-regulatory skills.

Parents indicated that they have reframed how they perceived their children's actions. They have stopped viewing their actions as annoying and evil and now see their children's negative reactions as opportunities to train and help them be better persons. Parents also felt that INSIGHTS took away some of the "ignorance and madness" experienced by the parent in child-rearing. Additionally, parents admitted to "talking more" rather than "shouting". They used strategies such as "giving time out" and employed the contract to arrive at an agreement with the children on a solution for correcting behaviours that are hard to change. In essence, the INSIGHTS programme enhanced the parent-child relationship.

Summary

This chapter reported results from the quantitative and qualitative analyses of data collected from parents during the intervention or at the end of the ten-week intervention. The data collected revealed the benefits that participants felt they derived from INSIGHTS and showed how parents disciplined their children's misbehaviour before participating in the intervention. The data collected at the end of the intervention for the various parents' groups show that Jamaican parents continue to use harsh discipline strategies. These strategies are unstructured and haphazard. In other words, parents did not put any thought into how to respond to their children's many behavioural problems.

Both the quantitative and qualitative data show that parents benefited from participating in the programme. The quantitative data showed that a high percentage of the parents felt that they learned new information and found the information helpful. The qualitative expanded on the quantitative by detailing the specific content sections, which were helpful and why. Content such as (1) learning about differences in children characteristics, (2) the importance of self-awareness and (3) the three categories to use in assessing their response to children: counterproductive, adequate and optimal. Parents had several recommendations for the intervention. Two of the five recommendations are the programme should be aired on television and the information displayed in an exhibition to the broader community.

8. The Influence of INSIGHTS on Teaching Practices

Teaching practice is the period that teachers spend at school in the pursuit of teaching students. Teaching in the classroom is not just about imparting content knowledge of a subject area, but it also includes interactions between teachers and students that involve real-time decisions and responses that facilitate students' academic and emotional development. Though teachers cannot directly alter the social background of students, teachers are in a position to place students' aggressive behaviour in perspective and thus create an environment that reduces aggression in the classroom (Jones and Jones 2015).

Teachers' classroom management practices and interactions influence students' academic and social skills, reduce children's disruptive and aggressive behaviours, improve the learning process, reduce teachers' stress and burnout and improve teacher-student relationships. Healthy teacher-students' relationships are "characterised by warmth, trust and low-degree of conflict" (Chamundeswari 2013; Baker, Grant and Morlock 2008, 3). Baker, Grant and Morlock reported that such attributes were associated with positive school outcomes. Teachers' classroom management practices also allow students to develop healthy socio-emotional characteristics. For example, Coplan and Prakash (2003) found that children at the early childhood stages of development who have aggressive tendencies would initiate more interactions with their teachers because of rejection by their peers; these children were more emotionally dependent on their teachers than their peers. On the other hand, those students who were less aggressive established a more secure relationship with teachers and were more "capable of using the teacher as a secure base and a resource for exploring social relationship with their peers, as well as learning opportunities in the classroom" (154). As teachers are exposed to strategies that enhance their behavioural management skills, they are more likely to help children be less dependent on their adult relationships and more inclined to explore their school environment and potential peer relationships.

Interventions and professional development workshops have helped teachers become aware of certain teacher practices or behaviours' potential negative or positive effects. These teacher development programmes in early childhood advance knowledge and skills on the assumption that information is dynamic and promotes high-quality professional practices "by enhancing systems and individuals to engage in activities that are self-sustaining and growth-producing" (Sheridan, Pope Edwards et al. 2009, 380).

The INSIGHTS into Children's Temperament intervention assists teachers in recognizing and understanding children's temperaments which influence differences in their behaviours. One of the intervention goals is to enhance teachers' potential to provide support for children's social-emotional development and academic improvement at the early childhood stage. Several studies (McClowry et al. 2010; Cappella et al. 2015; McCormick et al. 2014) discussed earlier reported that the INSIGHTS programme influenced teaching practices in the early childhood classroom. For example, following the INSIGHTS intervention, McClowry et al. (2010) reported that:

Teachers in INSIGHTS, compared to those in the Read Aloud programme, were 3.6 times more likely to report fewer problems managing boys' emotional-oppositional behaviour, 3.9 times more likely to report fewer problems with their attentional difficulties, and 5.5 times more likely to report less difficulty handling their covert disruptive behaviour. These findings support the assertion that teachers perceived themselves as more efficacious in handling disruptive classroom behaviour [following the INSIGHTS intervention]. (31)

What INSIGHTS Revealed about Teachers Practices Prior to Intervention

Before the INSIGHTS programme, teachers admitted to using inappropriate discipline strategies in their early childhood classroom. The discipline strategies (shouting, shaming, corporal punishment) that teachers echoed highlighted their misunderstanding of the overarching goal of discipline. The goals of discipline are to develop and train children to manage their own emotions and actions for the good of themselves and others. Instead, teachers used harsh discipline strategies to instil fear in students so that they could exert power in the classroom, reinforced by parents' indifference. One teacher voiced, while others nod their heads in agreement: "I used to outburst and run dem to dem [to their] seat."

Before being involved in INSIGHTS, teachers admitted to shaming children by putting children when they were "rude in front of the classroom while singing 'shame on you'". Also, teachers would inadvertently use corporal punishment. They voiced:

> One of the examples that I use in my classroom behaviour management strategy is to place the child at the front and sing "shame on you", when the child is not behaving. So, that is not really the biggest one, cause the biggest one is to take the child to the principal, and I think that is what she was trying to; so it's the behavioural steps.

> I just punished them (two slaps/corporal punishment).

> Well, not her in terms of being specific. Everybody is trying to move away from corporal punishment. I think children still need to get a little slap every now and then to know that you still know what they are up to. But I'm working my way out of that one. I don't do it much at school, but I tell my children I think you are bigger than that. However, if you don't want to follow what is happening, you are going to get something.

Teachers' thoughts and perceptions about a child in the moment of aggressive or disruptive behaviour will influence their reaction or response to the child. Teachers can choose how they perceive these moments, as teachable opportunities, or they can perceive the moments as burdensome. For example, teachers voiced that they viewed the students as rude, annoying and downright out of order. Teachers' expectations for children's behaviour at the early childhood level did not align with their developmental level. Teachers commented:

> I just thought that these children were downright "out of order".

> They don't know how to behave. [Teachers' expectations for children at the early childhood level]

> I thought that they were lazy and they needed to go back to basic school or stay home with their parents.

> Just thought they were rude children who didn't know how to sit still. Very annoying at times, they like to complain, not finishing their work on time, not doing the tasks given. It was very frustrating at times. [Teachers' expectations for children at the early childhood level]

There was a general agreement among all the participants that the government's ministry responsible for education in the country disrupts teaching practice with its policies and does not provide sufficient support in educating teachers about the various alternatives in-classroom behavioural management:

> [The] ministry have always been saying "no flogging" and stuff in school, yet they are not giving us the different option on how to discipline children.

It was also evident that teachers encountered difficulties in dealing with shy students. Teachers admit to ignoring shy children because they are not talkers, and as teachers, they are not equipped to interact with them. It was said,

> You may see an individual that who may be withdrawn and you try to go out of your way and help but you can't help because they are not talking to you; you don't know how to deal with them. And so you cater to the students who were participating. The ones that are not participating, they get lost because you don't know what they know. They are not talking to you; you talk to them, or you might shout at the class, and they may decide that they are not talking any more.

In the following sections, teachers shared their insights on how the programme enhanced their teaching practices. For example, teachers were guided in reframing how they viewed children's negative behaviours and increased their tools for managing student behaviours in the classroom. Teachers also observed that students' problem-solving skills improved during and after the INSIGHTS intervention.

Teachers' Feedback on the Influence of INSIGHTS Intervention

Overall, the quantitative revealed that teachers were not as positive towards INSIGHTS as the parents. There are two possible reasons for this – first, the teachers are trained educators, so the concept of temperament may not be new. The teachers may have had a theoretical understanding of the principles even though, in practice, they have not been applying the principles. And secondly, many of the teachers expressed concerns about the additional time and readings required by INSIGHTS. Hence teachers had to carry their regular workload and the additional time commitment of two hours per week to attend sessions plus additional readings from the programme. The following quantitative results were generated from weekly assessments for each two-hour weekly session conducted for eight weeks. The INSIGHTS team facilitated these sessions.

How Often Did You Use What You Learnt in INSIGHTS?

Approximately 49 per cent of the responses suggest that teachers often used the information learnt in INSIGHTS (see figure 8.1).

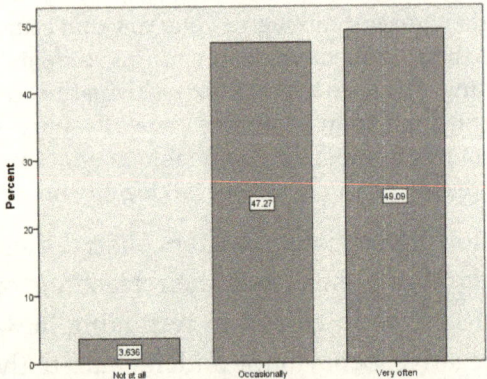

Figure 8.1: How often did teachers use what they learnt in INSIGHTS?

How much did you learn?

Approximately 41 per cent of the responses indicated that teachers felt that they learnt – this reflects the category in the figure – new information (see figure 8.2).

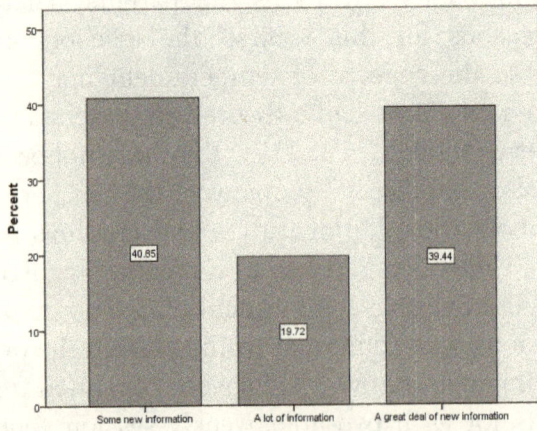

Figure 8.2: How much did teachers learn?

How useful was the new information you received?

Approximately 42 per cent of the responses suggest that teachers felt the new information received was extremely useful (see figure 8.3).

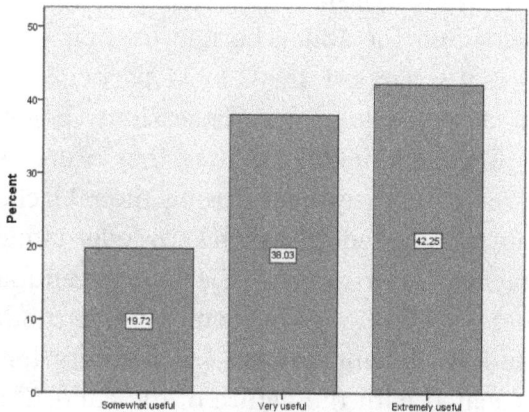

Figure 8.3: How useful was the new information teachers received?

How effective was your facilitator?

Approximately 49 per cent of the responses suggest that teachers rated their facilitator as very effective (see figure 8.4).

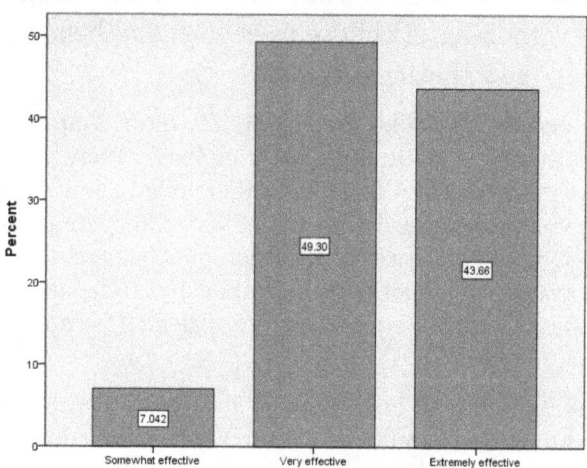

Figure 8.4: How effective was the teachers' facilitators?

Temperament: A Concept Learned in Teacher-training

The qualitative results expanded on the quantitative results by detailing how teachers felt about the intervention. Even though some teachers were resistant to the intervention because of the time factor and the added burden to their workload (the qualitative results support this), most participating teachers involved in the focus group discussions benefited from INSIGHTS. Teachers indicated that they were exposed to knowledge about temperament during their teacher training period but not to the extent that such knowledge influenced their teaching practice. After the INSIGHTS intervention, teachers reported that INSIGHTS gave them a better understanding of the definition of temperament, as teachers temperament was not associated with the nature of the child. Teachers can now reframe how they view students' disruptive behaviour in knowing this information. They can see how temperament can mediate the expected social and emotional skills teachers have for children at the early childhood level. By the end of INSIGHTS, teachers should recognize that no temperament is ideal in every situation; what is easy for children with certain temperaments is hard for children with other temperaments. Teachers reframing of children's challenging behaviours were reflected in the following comments:

> Yes, because just like how I didn't know that a child's temperament is naturally a part of them, there are other persons out there that don't know that information, especially when you have to deal with the children that are located in the geographical area that we teach in. Those persons need to be aware of the fact that the child is not rude, or naughty, that the child is just expressing his or herself because that is natural to him.

> Not really. I knew that some of the children are shy and some are grumpy and so on. But to say they were low-impact persistent or high in negative reactivity, no. The programme has taught me those terms.

I knew of them [referring to temperament], but the way they were categorize and the way they were highlighted helped me to better understand and identify them and, therefore, I have a better concept of what to expect from what kind of child, and how to best achieve their ultimate learning outcome.

INSIGHTS has reinforced some of the things that we have been doing, as well as giving us knew ideas and new strategies in dealing with a child, to accept what a child's temperament is. That he or she was born that way and it is natural for a child to behave in a certain way without being called naughty or rude. Programme opened my eyes.

INSIGHTS Enabled the Practical Application of the Principles of Temperament

The INSIGHTS programme facilitated a better understanding of children's temperaments and enabled the practical application of the principles of children's temperament to managing children's behaviours and negative reactions. Teachers reported that the programme helped them to identify their students' temperament types and to respond accordingly. After the programme, teachers were able to retrospectively note that their responses to their students before the programme were counterproductive and inappropriate:

> I will be able to apply what I learnt in my classroom. In that, understanding more about my students' temperament will help me to cater to their different learning styles.

> Excited, I have learnt a lot. It has opened my eyes to the children's temperament and why they behave in certain ways and how I'm to react to them, so that it doesn't come out negative and to help them also to understand and to make them know how to behave.

> So when a child is showing a different temperament we can really recognize it and deal with it in a manner where the child feel comfortable than we as teachers who did not understand, or the problem is there, but we couldn't recognize it, but we are now able to recognize it and deal with it, and so the child and the children can feel comfortable and not feel embarrass when we recognize the problem.

Yes, to some extent, because we already knew that children, everybody was different in some sort of way. But the programme give us an open eye to understand that some students are not rude, but they act a way because of their temperament. So, we were just seeing temperament as just the person's personality. We weren't seeing it in terms of their emotion.

I have twenty-four students in my class and you know most children are not alike; they are unique, they come with different personalities, different environment, and different background, so no children are the same. As a teacher, I thought that I couldn't manage my set of children; I couldn't deal with their dilemmas and all of that. But getting into this INSIGHTS programme have cause me now to be better able to deal with them and to be better able to manage them. So I think it's a good thing because it has allowed us to be more aware of things and better able to solve certain situation and to manage them.

Yes, I was able to accepts the student behaviour before, but sometimes it kinda give you a bit of frustrated feelings, but the programme has helped and sensitize us to more understand students' temperaments, and we have new ways of dealing with their situations. And it kinda make learning much more easier for us and then the students in turn; it's kinda umm, kinda help us as well to understand them more and understand ourselves more.

OK. We have children in our school from different environment. So you see children coming in with different temperament, and we, as teachers, we are early childhood teachers and not primary school or high school. These are babies and when they come in with their different temperaments, we as early childhood teachers, we have to recognize them, and we did not know how to recognize these problems. But since we have our facilitator who comes in with this programme, showed us the way how to recognize these problems, then we are able handle it better with these little ones. So, for the ones that are coming in now, it will be much easier for us as facilitator to recognize and understand the problem.

Well, I feel more at ease, more knowledgeable about the different temperaments in children, so am better able to deal with and help them with their problem-solving.

Another thing that I have discovered is, is the different temperaments, the withdrawal, the active, the task persistence, and all those things, and then the temperament profiles. Now the one that fascinates me is Frederico, that is, Frederico, that friendly personality because you see it happen so regular in society where children are lured away and it never dawn on me that this is a temperament profile they have that maybe cause it sometime, because I remember the child downtown that was lured away because of some patty business or something, and it just came back to me that, maybe, if we knew about something like what we know in this programme, then the children, maybe, would have been told that, "look, although you are friendly and although you would like to do this, there are dangers in doing so, so you don't go there, or you don't do this".

I just thought that they were just being rude. But since coming to the programme they have learnt a lot and I have learnt a lot. I said, "okay this person has this temperament, that person has that temperament". I'm able to make special provisions for those students.

I think I am now more competent in managing the behaviours, dealing with their temperaments, because I now understand it better, what to expect from, and temperament the child is displaying in their initial utterances. So, come September, in the beginning of the new term, I will be better able to manage my classroom, dealing with children, because I would be more exposed to what the temperaments are and how to manage them.

Change of Teachers' Perception of Children's Negative Behaviour

Whereas, before the training, teachers regarded students as "rude or downright out of order" and, therefore, gave harsh feedback to their students, teachers were now more understanding of their role when disciplining a child. INSIGHTS helped teachers change how they perceived their students and thereby allowed teachers to become more tolerant of their students' negative behaviours and use these opportunities as teachable moments. Teachers became more conscious of preparing their students for the next developmental level – the transition from infant to primary school. Teachers expressed their changed viewpoints:

> I would definitely recommend this programme to everybody, especially in basic schools where you know they are moving on to primary schools. So you know they will need this particular insight to deal with their own temperament and solve issues with another student. So you know bringing it to the bigger school where you have more people and bigger students. This will help them to solve their own issues, so I will recommend this to anybody. This is very good.

> Well, we were talking about the scaffolding. For this first term, we were doing a whole lot of workshops and our students were being supervised by different teachers, so a child might misbehave or act up on a particular day and you may discipline the child. Before now, I said the child was rude or whatever. After this programme, I said the child was thrown into the situation and might have been reacting to the new situation or the new teacher. So, it helps with how you deal with the child and things you put in place when you are going to be absent. As teachers, don't tell your child when you are not at school. Now you tell your children, "I will not be here tomorrow, or I might be late, Ms Saunders will be here, you know you are supposed to behave yourself, and I'll know what to do when I get back".

> Yes, because, just like how I didn't know that a child's temperament is naturally a part of them, there are other persons out there that don't know that information, especially when you have to deal with the children that are located in the geographical area that we teach in. Those persons need to be aware of the fact that the child is not rude, or naughty. That child is just expressing his or herself because that is natural to him. Help people to increase their understanding and develop ways and strategies to help them to deal with them. It can be frustrating when a child displays certain behaviours and you are not the mother or the father and you have to deal with it on a daily basis and you can't be bothered. But when you learn that the child is low in task, you have to develop ways to motivate them. It will be helpful. I give it a high 5.

INSIGHTS-trained Teachers to Respond, Not React

Teachers confessed that, before the programme, they would do or say anything thoughtlessly in response to the students' negative behaviour. However, subsequent to the programme, they have become more aware of the need to control their tempers by pausing before responding and thinking carefully about the situation before reacting:

> Before I react, I would think about it now. At first, I would just do anything and say anything, but now it has opened my eyes to what to do, what to say, and what not to do.

> I feel more relax within myself, and I feel more comfortable within myself, to know that I have been in the programme and it has change my whole, entire way of controlling the children. It makes me feel more relax because I can easily come in, even though sometimes they are so disordered and so forth. I can come in, sit and don't feel that anger inside of me. I feel more relax and I can come in and sit down and talk with them. You find that they are more attentive and seem more relax and ready for whatever is going to be said to them. So I feel more comfortable now with this programme, now that it is coming to an end.

INSIGHTS Students Promoted to Grade 1 Now More Manageable

Grade 1 teachers also noted a change in the behaviour of their students who were promoted from infant/basic to the grade 1 level. These teachers strongly felt that these students who participated in the INSIGHTS programme were more manageable. Also, teachers who participated in the programme were more competent in managing students in the classroom:

> As she said, the ones that are coming over [promoted from infant school to primary school, starting in grade one], they are more fit and able to manage them, and manage them better than how we use to before, because the programme has helped us to see where we went wrong. So, this is a correction, a correction on how to deal with and to manage the children

that are coming over, and how to manage the different temperaments can help us.

Improvement in Teachers' Relationships with Parents

Teachers reported that the programme improved their relationships with their students' parents. They found the use of the contract especially beneficial, as it provided guidance on how to effectively engage both parents and students in discussions. Teachers were encouraged to develop contracts for their students, including their parents if problem behaviours occurred at home and school. The contract allows parents and teachers to work with a child in resolving a problem behaviour; all three persons sign the contract when negotiation is completed. Teachers voiced:

> Another thing is the parent relationship. I didn't even know how effective it would be just to sign a contract with that child, because I have done it in my class based on the programme and it is working.

> Yes, there is a lot of information in the presentations that will help parents and teacher to deal with their children. The programme helps with the acceptance of each other.

> At this school, we're gonna do a session [on contract] with all the teachers, and September everybody should know how they can deal with the parents' behaviour, you know, and how they can deal with the children, cause as I said, everybody's behaviour is different, and we need to learn how to appreciate and work with it. Just know that person, how that person behaves, and so we just need to work along, it might not be that the person is rude or want to be rude, but it's just the person's personality. So, we'll just work with it, and things, hopefully, will be better.

> The most difficult aspect of the programme for me, outside of me identifying my teaching and working on them, was to get parents on board. I find that, at this stage, a lot of parents don't think it's necessary to be very involved in the child's development and they tend to leave it to the teachers, and

that's where the major challenge comes from. The negative aspect of the temperament are coming from their own child's frustration with what is happening around them, and the fact that they feel like it's them against the world or them against teachers because this is not what teachers are looking for and am not getting it at home. I think, for the most part, it helps to know that the parents understand the children better and, therefore, you get more positive responses and beneficial results from doing this programme [Teachers were aware that there were sessions for parents running parallel to theirs in the school].

The teachers' reports revealed the impact the programme had on the children's behaviour in school. The children received training in solving dilemmas and learned strategies to respond to difficult situations through the programme. Teachers gave anecdotal evidence of changes in their students' behaviour resulting from their classroom management strategies due to their participation in the INSIGHTS programme. The teachers said:

They know their classmate's temperament, they are better able to deal with situations in the class. They will say, "Miss, a dilemma happen", and I will ask, "how did you deal with it?, which is the best strategy to use"?

I had a little boy in my class and, for the life of me, I couldn't get any work out of him and a couple children. Well, there was this one particular girl, I'd say to her, "bring your book to the table let me see what's happening". And she is not coming to me, and when I go to her she urinates on herself. I'm wondering what is this child's problem. So, I didn't pay her any mind. I just decided to chill. And then I met another little boy. He is in my class. This is second term but, since this programme, this boy has transformed. Giving problem, up and down, and he was never that sort of child. Then, I realized that he was the Coretta type, very shy. I used some of the strategies, and he has changed. I realized that, before this, I may have been causing a lot of blockage for students. Because he did not communicate with me much last school term. Since this programme, he always has something to share, so I have to tell him "all right you can sit". He is running, breaking all rules. This boy used to sit down and I don't even know he is there. It helps for both teachers and students.

Additionally, teachers' relationships with their students improved as teachers' frustrations were minimized. The INSIGHTS strategies increased the tools available for use in behavioural management in the classroom. The teachers noted:

> Yes, I have accepted it in terms of knowing how to better work with them. I can identify the different temperaments. I signed contracts with the children which really helps them to improve the behaviours that need improvement.

> The methods/strategies that I used before, I try my very best to eliminate them, or use them less, and started to develop more ways to address them. In terms of using the contracts, setting goals with them and working alongside them, allowing them to decide the consequence for their behaviour in a way that would be beneficial to them. Not just to stop the behaviour, but to allow a growth in the process or a form of development, so it would benefit me, as well as them. This is what I try to do now in terms of using less counterproductive), and I try to use more optimal strategies because now that I have learnt that temperament is a part of the child, and the child is unique in their own way, I try to use strategies that help them to grow and understand that even though this is a part of them, it is not acceptable in this situation. It's a growing process.

> The programme is quite an informative one. We have learnt a lot how to deal with the different temperaments of children, and it has better help me to relate to the different temperament experience in the classroom.

> Ok, wow. Well, I wish the programme would last a little bit longer. I really enjoy it and, although it has ended, I have learnt a lot and will implement the strategies I have learnt in this classroom, and it help me also to accept each child, and help and remind me that each child is unique, and I should use different strategies.

Some teachers extended the application of the principles of INSIGHTS to their homes. For example, a teacher echoed the following:

Well, I feel more equipped and better able to deal with and manage these temperaments. I now know exactly what to do, not only [have I] become even calmer in certain situations [but I can] apply it to [my] personal life too. You have children and their different temperaments. You can also apply it to your children.

The Most Useful Sections of the Programme

Several teachers found the sessions interesting because of the ways in which the facilitators engaged participants with the content of the programme and the teaching and learning strategies that were embedded in the programme. Focus group participants commented on the most useful sections of the programme:

> Interviewer: Okay. What was the interesting part of the programme? Can you think of any part?
>
> Focus group: Listening to the facilitator.
>
> Interviewer: Listening to the facilitator?
>
> Focus group: Because of how she brought across the information. She ensured that we understood. She repeated herself to ensure that we were grasping, that it was really getting where it should, and then she used her vignettes to reinforce and gave us homework.

The INSIGHTS programme provided participants with ready access to critical principles of the programme for review and consolidation:

> We have handouts, so we can go back, and the information delivered good, and we have notes and jottings, and so we can always refer to and so.

Similar to the parents, the teachers were trained to assess their responses to their students before enactment. They found the three criteria for assessing their responses – inadequate, adequate and optimal – quite helpful. They commented:

> Since the programme, we try to use a lot of optimal responses. So, it helps us to be more alert with our responses to the children. Not that we weren't doing it, we were, but in our subconscious we try to be a better teacher and apply what we have been taught. We like Session 3: Teacher Responses – optimal, adequate and counterproductive responses.
>
> It is amazing to see that I have used the counterproductive response on several occasions. But I have now learnt that the counterproductive should not be used, although there are instances when it will have to be used. I am now learning that that response does not really work; it actually makes the situation worse.
>
> This is what I try to do now in terms of using less counterproductive, and I try to use more optimal strategies because now that I have learnt that temperament is a part of the child and the child is unique in their own way I try to use strategies that help them to grow and understand that even though this is a part of them, it is not acceptable in this situation. It's a growing process.
>
> The part I like the most is the responses section. I was able to identify them very quickly in terms of the adequate response, the optimal and the counterproductive.

The programme deepened the teachers' understanding of various behavioural management strategies applicable to children's behaviour. It thus made the students more responsive to the disciplinary actions of the teachers. The teachers noted:

> Right, right, yes. Doing this programme has opened my eyes to doing something like this. Giving recognition is another thing. I used to do it, but just to ... per se. I did not know enough behind it, and how effective it could be. What I have learnt is that the more recognition you give, the more it encourages other children to come on board in doing good things. Sorry about that [the teacher seems to be apologizing about his/her lack of knowledge]. The programme has helped me in such a way that I am supposed to be able to guide my age group a little better and show them how to, how to give recognition to each other, how to appreciate each other's feelings and how to be a bit more kinder to each other. The programme has provided me with all the information that I needed to do this.

The use of contracts for behaviours that teachers found particularly annoying and repetitious allowed the teachers to focus less on the child's negative behaviour and more on nurturing the child's development: "In terms of using the contracts – setting goals with them and working alongside them, allowing them to decide the consequence for their behaviour in a way that would be beneficial to them. Not just to stop the behaviour, but to allow a growth in the process or a form of development, so it would benefit me as well as them" (INSIGHTS MANUAL).

The teachers greatly appreciated the comprehensive nature of the INSIGHTS programme and felt that the programme allowed for the improvement of parent-teacher, teacher-child and parent-child relationships. Several teachers voiced the following: "It doesn't just target the behaviour at school, but also at home. So, it work with the parent, and it help us to work with the parent to help to control the children at home as well as school. So, when we correct the behaviour at school, you know it's been corrected at home too" (INSIGHTS MANUAL).

INSIGHTS programme emphasizes rewards and recognition along with the contracts. For example, one teacher shared about the collaborative contract where the parents and teacher collaborated with the children to achieve specific goals:

> I can attest to two boys from my class in which I have seen some change in behaviours; so it is on the parents and the teachers to follow through. For one of the boys, usually he doesn't do his work, and so I wanted him to do it and so, in the morning when I come, I would show him the reinforces, like the stars and the smiley faces, and so he will be on task. He will finish his work on time, get it really neat so he can get his star in his book, and also on the contract that we have, so he is also looking forward for that, so he always get his work neatly done. At home, his mother always encourages him, "if you go to school and you do your work nice and you behave yourself, when you come home you will get and additional sticker". So he always work toward my sticker, plus the additional sticker from his mother.

> The use of the contract also worked well because the children, being a part of the actual agreement, children tried their best to do well in order to fulfil their part of the agreement.

Similar to the parents, teachers felt the audio-visual vignettes shown during the programme were effectively delivered:

> I like the use of the technology and how it helped me to connect what it was that I was learning to my everyday situation. I also enjoyed the look of the dramatization in the students' sessions that helped them to make connections with the learning, what they were learning, how to manage their temperament, how to recognize the temperament of other children and how to be better able to assist in situations that cause for dilemma.

Teachers' Observations of the Effects of INSIGHTS on the Students

Parallel to the teacher-parent sessions, the students age five and above years participated in ten thirty-minute sessions on a weekly basis in their schools. During this time, students learnt to celebrate their uniqueness through discussions on the different personality types and accept each other's differences. They also learnt about conflict management by problem-solving in the event of a dilemma. The adults who participated in the study reported the effects of the programme on the children. The teachers noted that the students experienced improved competency in problem-solving and word recognition. In addition, the teachers observed that students started to exhibit an understanding of differences:

> Allowing them [students] to solve their own dilemmas, sometimes you watch them solving their own dilemma. Like yesterday, myself and another teacher sat there and watch a couple of students solve their own dilemma, and we were sitting, not saying anything, and they solve it without any intervention from us. So it's good, you nuh, the strategies that they use to solve their own dilemmas, and the strategies she [the facilitator] taught us, even here, when she teach them the strategies, they use it over there, and they find out what is a dilemma and solve it on their own.

> It's very useful for the students, and they are able to express themselves, breaking down the problem-solving.
>
> Yes, for the children, they know what a dilemma is. They were taught what is a dilemma and they know it is a big problem, and they know how to solve it, to recognize the problem, think and try out. So, they know how to do it unuh from there. You don't have to really intervene if they are having a dilemma outside [the classroom]. They will come and complain and then we will say, "well you have learnt it, so you know how to solve it, so go and try it out and then come back to us", and that's what they did. It may not be that perfect, but you know they are trying and you can see that they understand what they have learnt.
>
> The children are able to solve their own problems. If they have issues on the playfield, they don't come to check with me during lunchtime.

In the programme, students learn sight words that expand their vocabulary. These sight words are core concepts in each lesson. For example, some teachers create a word wall in their classroom with INSIGHTS words along with different images of the puppets.

So, it is not just about the behaviour; these children learn these big words. Word recognition. They know it anywhere – temperament, cautious and guess what, they know the meaning, and another thing is that she [the facilitator] allows them to talk. She allows them to express themselves, for instance, they are having the discussion on dilemma, she asks, "what is a dilemma?" and they are able to express themselves and tell what it is. Each week, she'll ask, "Who has a dilemma this week"?, and so the child becomes familiar with the word and understands what the whole concept is about.

> So, they can look and say "so and so" is grumpy. "Miss, we had a dilemma today"; they talk about it all the time.
>
> The children love it and they remember all the characters and they match it to the classmates. I think they should come back and do the other grade ones and the Junior High Department.

Challenges with the Programme

1. Time

The major challenge aired by teachers regarding the INSIGHTS programme was the duration of the programme, both in terms of the ten weeks and the two hours' weekly sessions. Some teachers reported difficulties in allocating time to attend the two-hour sessions as this meant finding someone to attend to their students while they were involved with the sessions. In addition, several teachers found the programme intrusive and demanding:

> Regardless of the fact that the programme gives us an eye-opener, mi glad seh it finish because it is time consuming and it kinda infringe on our time. However, the good part of it is that we have seen some benefits because we are better able to deal with the children, and I feel justified knowing that whatever we do with them, we are doing it fairly.

> My biggest difficulty was leaving my class at one o'clock to come to the session cause then I have to find somebody to take them [the students] for that time. So, maybe then, miss, in my opinion, I would prefer if it starts when school really dismisses and then most of the children are gone home. So, maybe a two o'clock thing would be a little better, in a sense. I am thinking of the summer and am thinking of bus fare and getting out of the house if I'm at home and so forth. I sorta more have the feeling for it while I am at school.

> The timing to come to the sessions. You have to go to class and give out homework and then you can't be bothered to come here for so many hours. The timing was the biggest part of it.

> In the evenings I am a bit exhausted after a long day. I have to tell myself that it's beneficial for me as well as the children that are in my care. So, I have to put out the effort to try and stay back. The day is long and we have so much to do in the day. The most difficult part is to stay back in the evening.

> The timing, that was the most difficult part and getting the children to work in their text book. It kinda clash with what we want to do with our curriculum. To find the time to get

them to actually do the activities in the workbook was a bit of challenge, but it was done.

2. Homework

In addition to the time spent attending each session, INSIGHTS also gave a written assignment to reinforce the strategies for each session. Teachers also expressed the view that the homework assignments after each weekly session were taxing:

> The most difficult part of the programme, OK, to tell the truth, homework. Sometimes, let me speak softly, "lol", I am very tired, like having twenty-four or twenty-five children in the class on a daily basis, I tell you, they drain us. So, when we get homework in the afternoon, we can't manage, it's too hard, why? Because we can't find the time. We not even have the time for our own children at home, and every day we get homework, enuh. But, guess what, we get our homework and we got correction. First of all, we learn that in the last part here we apply what we learnt. I think the part that we didn't like most was the homework part and then to study for the test.
>
> Less literature, yes, for us to do, like the homework. It was a bit challenging. I would recommend to limit the assignment as well because they don't get enough time to complete them, and we could have like parents, teachers session where parents come in and talk to the teachers.
>
> Yes, as she said, the homework was a bit hectic and tedious, very tedious…But the good thing about it is because we have the insight on what to do when we come the day, I can do the homework and she can sit and look at it and say then OK, "this is the correction" and "this is not the correction". The test, for the test, I don't think I did study for the test, but I know a little thing through learning from the training I knew and apply it.

3. Dependency on School Resources

During the initial stages of the implementation of the INSIGHTS programme, technical equipment was not provided, and the programme had to depend on the resources of the schools. Over time, the programme received funds from CHASE, which helped alleviate the demand for the schools' equipment. Nevertheless, the INSIGHTS team continued to face challenges, especially finding a fixed room in the schools. Several schools struggled to provide a physical facility for the programme. One INSIGHTS team member stated:

> The most difficult part of the programme was to prepare for it, because we had to, like, set up. We don't have a space for where these equipment are set up, the overhead projector and so. So, we had to makeshift to facilitate the programme. Sometimes we were in the classroom, sometimes we were in the library, at other times we were in the board building, we were in the computer rooms, you understand? So, sometimes we had to make shift to facilitate it.

Teachers' Recommendation for the INSIGHTS Programme

The teachers recommended the following for the programme:

- Extending the INSIGHTS programme to the secondary school level – we need to bring it up there. Just as we have sessions with the five years olds, we have a group of teenagers – maybe fourteen, fifteen. Have that session with them. I think it will help because they need to know about this temperament dilemma and how to handle certain situations. They need to know. The teachers need to understand also.

- Implement INSIGHTS at the beginning of the academic year not in the middle of the academic year – if we are doing this programme, we want to see result at the end of it, and we want it to be a lifetime opportunity for the children. We don't want to start it and stop in mid-year, so I believe that April to June timing is not a good timing. For me, it would be between September/October, and we will follow through, throughout the year if possible.

- INSIGHTS should not be restricted to a specific grade (The teachers shared the sentiment that the programme should not be restricted to specific grades but should be extended to the entire school community) – Yes, I would recommend it to the entire school, not just grade 1.
- INSIGHTS should start at the earlier ages in the basic or infant schools – we get students starting from four years old, and the earlier they learn how to manage their own temperament for teachers to deal with them, the better.

Currently, the INSIGHTS programme starts with the five-year-olds and extends to seven-year-olds. Several teachers believed that the programme should started earlier with younger students and extend into the secondary schools.

Puppets

The programme has large puppets representing each temperament displayed during the sessions. Along with these large-sized puppets were the hand puppets (which the children used during role-playing and dramas), with the images of the four puppets representing the four temperament profiles. The teachers felt that the puppets could be more infused in the programme in a more effective and efficient manner. They voiced the following:

> Even for the children using the puppets, if they were able to manipulate using the one say, for example, Gregory, the Grumpy, and you have children behaving to act out who Gregory was like, I think they would enjoy it more, instead of watching and talking about it.

> I was thinking that they could have more puppets, because you know children love to interact with puppets, and puppets grab their attention. So, we could have puppets for an individual, each child having their own puppets. That would be good.

> Each child having their own puppets, even to take home, that would have been a good thing, because once they leave here, they can go back home and enact whatever was been taught or reinforce whatever have been taught.

Teachers' Conclusions

The INSIGHTS programme assisted in the overall development of the students, as well as that of the teachers. The teachers identified aspects of the programme that they liked, such as handling dilemmas, adherence to the contracts and the disciplinary steps. They noted:

> The programme not only highlights the child's temperament, but it reviews other areas of the student within the classroom. It helps the teacher to reinforce good practices, like how they respond to the children, how they deal with punishment, and even to be in the classroom, to listen to the children and show empathy, how to be assertive and to give recognition, and how to deal with conflict, and how to teach the children to deal with their own conflicts.

> Well, I feel more at ease, more knowledgeable about the different temperaments in children. So, I am better able to deal with and help them with their problem-solving.

> You are learning something new, and it is very encouraging to learn something new, so you can, maybe, pass it on to other student and teachers in the school. As I said, not everyone is apart, but as I said, it's encouraging, and you can help somebody else.

The INSIGHTS programme also revealed that teachers, like parents, use shame to discipline the children by shouting at them in front of their classmates and applying corporal punishment. Although the teachers were exposed to temperament theories during their teacher-training experience, the knowledge remained theoretical and did not influence their teaching practice. Some teachers declared that they did not know about temperament before the INSIGHTS programme. For these teachers, INSIGHTS enabled the practical application of the theoretical principles of temperament.

Through the programme, teachers were empowered to deal with students' differences and acknowledge that a one-size-fits-all is not an efficient nor effective classroom management approach and consider the uniqueness of the children in the classrooms. Additionally, teachers reframed their views of the children's negative reactions as "wicked and evil". They understood that various temperament has strengths and constraints and that it is the responsibility of the teachers to help students manage these constraints. Another result of the INSIGHTS programme is that the teachers became more sensitive and caring in managing their students' negative behaviours in the classroom. For example, the teachers started to view a student's display of "rudeness" as a powerful opportunity to train the child. Unlike the quantitative results, the focus group results for teachers revealed that the programme not only assisted the teachers in understanding children but also equipped them with tools and strategies for training the children, thereby increasing their classroom management skills.

Overall, INSIGHTS improved not only the teacher-student relationship but also teacher-parent relationships. Many teachers expressed that the programme should not be restricted to early childhood classrooms but should be expanded to primary and secondary schools. In helping teachers increase their classroom behaviour management competencies, the INSIGHTS programme also contributed substantially to the socio-emotional development of the children.

Summary

This chapter explored teachers' experience with INSIGHTS and how they felt the programme enhanced their behaviours management practices. We also reported on teachers' discipline strategies before participating in the intervention. Before entering INSIGHTS, the teacher spoke honestly about their tendency to use harsh discipline strategies, and they talked very harshly to them. Teachers voiced that they saw children's problem behaviour as annoying or downright out of order. Keep in mind that these teachers are responsible for elementary schoolchildren, yet they expect them to know how to behave.

In addition, this reflects the stress that our teachers face in the classroom.

The quantitative results revealed that the teachers were not as positive towards INSIGHTS as the parents. However, the qualitative results showed why their attitude towards INSIGHTS had challenges and what the teachers liked about the programme. Teachers felt that the demands on their time were too burdensome without any consideration for their regular working time.

Teachers felt that the programme helped them apply some of the principles they learned during their student-teacher training. Teachers felt that the programme helped them better understand temperament and how their temperament profile affects children's behaviour. The programme helped the teachers to reframe how they perceived children's problem behaviours. Most children are not rude and evil, but there are negative reactions in every temperament that must be managed. Hence children need to be taught by adults how to develop controls.

9. Facilitating Differences in Children's Development

Facilitating Differences in Children's Development

Children's personal strengths and constraints are challenged throughout their school years from early in their development both at school and at home. They face the looming threat of failure in the classroom and on the playground to meet teachers' and their peers' expectations. These expectations are imposed on them or those they set for themselves. For example, a five-year-old little boy observed that he is active and constantly compared with another child who can sit still and finish the assigned task by the teacher. His shortcomings can provoke shame from the teachers and teasing from his peers. Sometimes the price to be paid for being different can be modest or substantial (Levine 2002). This price must be paid when a child is forced to behave like someone else. The outcomes of mismatching a child's temperament with the environment as a daily occurrence can result in poorness of fit, resulting in undesirable consequences for the child and those within the environment. To build character through helping children to enhance their strengths and manage their constraints in their temperament requires that the teacher and parent understand the child (Levine 2002). The INSIGHTS programme is a practical tool that provides parents and teachers with behavioural management strategies that can be used to understand children and help them deal with dilemmas caused by the constraints of their temperaments. Several considerations have emerged from interacting and collecting data from the teachers and parents in the programme: the role of leadership in the schools for the sustainability of a programme; parents' honesty about their needs and their desire for change; the role of training teachers in creating goodness of fit environment to accommodate children's uniqueness; and fostering collaboration between teachers and parents in sustaining the principles of difference. This chapter also provides some guidelines for teachers and parents to be solution-oriented in their behavioural management practices.

School Leadership and Its Influence on the Sustainability of the Programme

Whereas we acknowledge the role of teachers in using meaningful discipline techniques that will create a goodness of fit environment for children with different temperaments in the classroom, school leadership is important in facilitating the sustainability of change in classroom management strategies. The empowerment of teachers to bring about change depends on the school leader. This was evident from our qualitative assessment of the sustainability of INSIGHTS in the school culture. Several schools licensed during the CHASE funding period as school-based facilitators of INSIGHTS continued with the programme even though the management team went into slow motion as funding came to an end.

During this transition period, the management team that took over INSIGHTS contacted the principals of the ten licensed schools. They indicated that the INSIGHTS strategies were still infused in teaching practices. We spoke with several other school leaders and realized that a principal's disposition towards a programme influenced sustainability. There were administrative excuses when asked about having INSIGHTS workshops in certain schools; in those schools, the effects of INSIGHTS dwindled. On the other hand, principals who were enthusiastic about INSIGHTS infused the strategies into their school culture. An exemplary school that continued during this period was Alpha Infant. When we contacted the principal and apologized for the non-activity of INSIGHTS for a short period with an invitation to do workshops for teachers and parents, the principal did not hesitate to accept. During COVID, the INSIGHTS team facilitated an eight-week workshop for teachers and parents; these were held at separate periods via Zoom at Alpha. The principal herself attended the teachers' sessions and attended the parents' session now and then.

Background Information to the School

Alpha Infant is part of a Roman Catholic institution that comprised an infant, primary and a single-sex high school for girls. The institution is in the central urban area of Jamaica. Alpha is a faith-based community that "fosters positive relationships among learners, teachers and parents". Alpha Infant School was started in August 1896 by the Roman Catholic Sisters to facilitate the education of children four to six years old. The school presently has three hundred students with a staff of approximately fourteen members. The primary school presently has a population of one thousand students. The primary was initially a preparatory school started 125 years ago. There are two principals: one for the infant school and one for the primary. The Alpha Infant School is a feeder school for the primary and, as the principal mentioned later, for Jesse Primary.

Alpha Infant is a member of the original cohort of schools that participated in the INSIGHTS at the programme's initial implementation in 2014. Remember from the previous chapters that the INSIGHTS sessions helped teachers and parents understand and celebrate differences in children's temperaments. The programme also provides strategies for young children to solve dilemmas in the classroom and on the playground.

Infusing INSIGHTS into the School Culture

The principal facilitated change through her decisions and actions. For example, she told us in an interview that there is a wall for INSIGHTS on the school compound (see figure 1); in addition, she commented:

> This is an alternative [referring to the INSIGHTS programme] that is proven and works, and we can say that, and we're not being paid to do that we are just impressed with the programme itself, and the fact that teachers are getting this kind of training allows them to cope even better in the classroom.

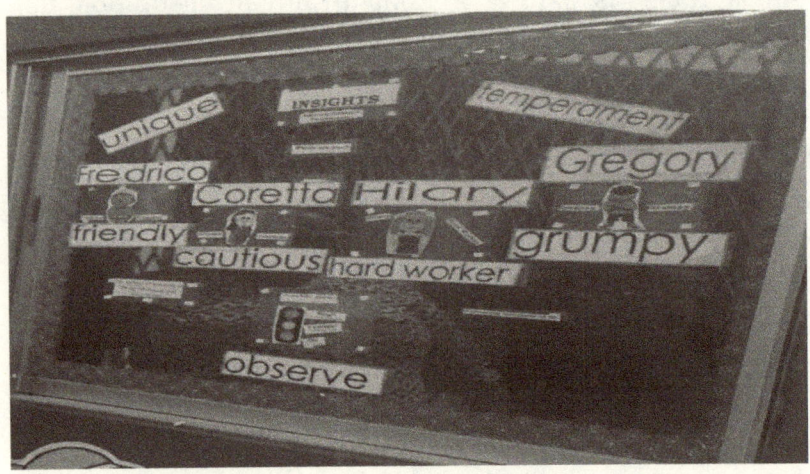

Figure 9.1: INSIGHTS Wall in Alpha School

Sustainability of INSIGHTS

The principal spoke to the sustainability of the principles of INSIGHTS. In the following excerpt, she indicated that the primary schools that children from Alpha Infant transition to notice the change in their children's behaviour over the years. This behaviour change is also highlighted when compared to children coming from other feeder schools:

> We [Alpha Infant] are linked with Jessie and Alpha Primary because we spend a lot of time in many workshops. And one of the things that principals share is that our students are calmer, less likely to get into altercations, they are more the mediators, okay? Yes, because you have a mixture going to primary school. So when the others come in, and we were telling them, it was the INSIGHTS programme, remember Alpha primary School had a little introduction to INSIGHTS. But that principal would have retired, some teachers left. But for every year, they get our students, they don't have the challenges as much because our children are more tolerable of others. They're more tolerable of their peers. Because they know don't get frustrated, easy... aggression doesn't come out as much we have seen this for over six years. We don't have fights and that's what is amazing about the programme, it's sustainable.

Teachers in a focus group discussion also reinforced the principal's comments. Teachers expressed that now that they are given additional tools of understanding and appreciating children's differences, they are less frustrated and harsh in their classroom management approach. They also indicated that the principles they learned in INSIGHTS were not restricted to their classroom. Still, several teachers used the INSIGHTS principles with their children at home and in another environment such as a church where they are responsible for children. For example, a teacher from Alpha Infant, who participated in a focus group discussion, shared:

> Alright, so for me, I just want to thank Mrs Foster [the principal]. I am glad I got the opportunity to have partake in INSIGHTS when I did. And so for me, it has been a positive one in terms of, I would be less frustrated, or less stern, after understanding or using what INSIGHTS has taught in understanding the temperament of the child. So you know, you'll be less, less strict after understanding the temperament of the child and learning the different methods that you can

use to bring about a positive change. So I really appreciate that I've gotten the opportunity to partake in INSIGHTS and to learn and to take away what I've learned to use in the everyday life, not only at school, but as I say I teach Sunday school and other things. So yes, I am grateful to INSIGHTS.

Principals play a critical role in bringing about and inspiring change in the classroom and the school community. They are not only the "pacesetter" but also the initiators of change; they prioritize the goals of the school's community. In bringing about change, the principal must exemplify change by being interested and connected to the activities for achieving the school's goals (Fullman 2020). Mrs Foster, the principal of Alpha Infant, was an example of such leadership. She believed in the principles of the programme; she admitted to using the INSIGHTS principles in her interactions not only with the children but also with parents and teachers.

The Significant Role of Teachers in Creating a Goodness of Fit Environment to Accommodate Children's Uniqueness

Jamaican teachers are authoritarian in their discipline approach. Because they are trained as educators and exposed to different approaches in classroom management, they are less reactive than parents. Jamaican teachers seem to value "respect for authority, respect for work, and respect for the preservation of order" (Baumrind 1971, 22). It was also evident from the focus group discussions and literature (Henningham-Baker and Walker 2009; Henningham-Baker et al. 2009; Harriott and Jones 2016) that teachers favour punitive and forceful measures. They believe that children should not question their standards but accept their word as the standard for right or wrong. Authoritarian teachers are not responsive to the children's needs and lack self-awareness and possible impact on the children. Though Jamaican teachers have this inclination toward authoritarian discipline strategies, they are open and dispose to change once given exposure to alternatives. Teachers who participated in INSIGHTS wanted continuous professional development. Henningham-Baker et al. (2009) observed that benefits to child behaviour were facilitated in part by the improvements in teachers' practices.

Teachers can be the first representation of the world outside the family that interacts with and facilitates interaction with young children. As the initial separation from parents can be difficult and traumatic for a child, teachers must take the responsibility of helping the child through this transition. As time progresses in the teacher-child relationship, the child sees the teacher as a surrogate parent. Teachers are, therefore, mediators in a child's interactions; how the teacher mediates will influence the child's development of skills in relating to others and society. Thus, the teachers should be knowledgeable about temperaments and the strengths and challenges of the different temperament profiles revealed by researchers and scientists. There are ample research articles and books on temperament to understand and help children with troublesome temperamental challenges.

Teachers enter the classroom with their experiences encountered throughout their lives. Their experiences with their parents, peers and teachers create imprints on their minds, influencing their actions and reactions in the classroom. As parents, some teachers use reactive measures to discipline children. Throughout the programme, teachers were informed that their responsibility is to create the type of environment that facilitates differences and maintains relationships. This environment is affected by the disciplinary strategies teachers administer to children when they misbehave. When teachers use reactive strategy, they "are more likely to respond negatively to students' inappropriate behaviours, rather than responding positively to students' appropriate behaviours" (Clunies-Ross, Little and Keinhuis 2008, 695).

In the teacher response session, teachers were presented with a list of indicators of counterproductive responses (nags, teases and lectures); adequate responses (taking command, ignoring, using signals to give warning); and the optimal response (encouraging children to consider ways to resolve their situations). Teachers also learnt how to recognize situations that may be temperamentally difficult. Following this, teachers decide on the degree of scaffolding activities for the child. INSIGHTS programme challenges teachers to focus not only on accomplishing the academic content of their profession but also on accepting their role in developing the students' characters by strengthening a relationship with the children they teach.

Parents Significant Role in Creating a Goodness of Fit Environment to Accommodate Children's Uniqueness

Jamaican parents do not have a mental framework of what type of parents they want to be. There are no goals or objectives in their decision to respond to their children's problem behaviours. They react to problem behaviours based on how they were parented as children. There is no assessment of the positives and negatives of their parental approach. Several pieces of literature support the findings of the results presented in this study. For example. Researchers such as Fernald and Meeks-Gardner (2003) and Burke and Kuczynski (2018) reported on the harsh parenting style of Jamaican parents. When children are resistant to parents' demands, they experience severe consequences for noncompliance. Parents interpret noncompliance as "disrespect and communicate emotions of annoyance, displeasure, resentment, scorn, impatience or disdain" (Burke and Kuczynski 2018, 8). Parents who participated in INSIGHTS were not shy in reporting their harsh discipline strategies. As one parent pointed out in the focus group, their parents disciplined them. Once parents who participated in INSIGHTS became aware that their harsh approach was not beneficial to their children, they expressed the desire to change because they wanted the best for their children. Not all parents were consistent in attending the session, but I would estimate that approximately 80 per cent of the parents maintained consistent attendance in a typical of ten parents; two parents would be absent.

During the INSIGHTS sessions, parents can present their viewpoints on how they would like their parenting to be. During these sessions, facilitators realize that parents underthink their role as parents and thus treat their children harshly. The INSIGHTS programme challenges parents to recognize that effective parenting is not acting on impulse but involves mental effort, that is, thinking. Thinking involves reasoning, using judgements to make decisions and using those decisions to determine actions.

During the INSIGHTS programme, parents learn to take responsibility for their actions. Several of the parents confessed that they shouted when correcting their children. When correcting a child, the parents learnt to look at the child's actions and be self-aware when correcting or disciplining a child. Parents also learnt that they do not have to be harsh in their disciplinary practices, but, as parents, they can reason with a child who is even as young as five years. A child may be similar to or different from the parent. Both similarities and differences can cause issues between parent and child. Parents are therefore invited, during the programme, to reflect on their personality and to assess the extent of their negative reactivity. The parents noted that the programme enhanced their awareness of their parental skills and behaviour through the Social Competences and Parental Responses Sections discussed earlier.

Of the eight social competencies that the programme targeted, parents reported that they benefited most from the sessions concerning listening. By the end of the programme, parents were motivated to understand their children and respond rather than react to their negative actions. Parents reported that they talked more and shouted less when their children displayed inappropriate behaviours. According to the INSIGHTS programme, listening is a process whereby parents focus on what their children are saying to them and actively demonstrate this by responding in a manner that indicates to the children that they are actively hearing. Active listening includes asking the child to repeat when they are not sure that they heard correctly or repeating what the child said to ensure they understood. Listening facilitates understanding and generates solutions to problems. Listening also allows parents time to calm the emotions which might be welling up inside and lowers their tendency to react by administering harsh disciplinary measures. Several parents reported that they understood their children's character and actions better by listening more to their children and shouting less. Parents were so enthusiastic about the training that teachers reported how encouraged they were to see how parents responded to change in the focus group. For example, the teacher pointed out that in a PTA meeting when a parent started complaining about her child, parents who attended eight weeks sessions reported:

> and when the parent started to complain two parents turned and said that's why you need to do the INSIGHTS programme. I was so impressed; the parents turn to the parents and say: so when is the other one [when is the next one]. Miss Foster, when can we sign up? The parents know that when their child does X, Y, Z, I use this strategy and the other one agreed and said, yes, INSIGHTS is working and more parents need to join INSIGHTS.

Strengthening Teacher and Parent's Relationship

The programme provides practical guidance to parents and teachers on how to collaborate for the child's good. The collaboration of parents and teachers can foster students' engagement in the learning process as parents and teachers can share notes on the challenges and reinforce the positive factors of the child's competencies in the learning process. Together parents and teachers can develop strategies to help the child tackle contrary but complementary challenges, which create and reinforce social skills and academic competence.

Parents and teachers reported that they started to respond rather than react to children's negative behaviours. Their communication with their children was enhanced; they realized that children are different from each other and that these differences should not be condemned but accepted and celebrated. The parents were also instructed on goal setting and were encouraged to set short- and long-term goals. Short-term goals were recommended for contracts between parents and children to resolve children's recurring behavioural problems that seem impossible to solve. The long-term goal is "intended to assist the child in making a habit of good behaviour" (*INSIGHTS Manual*, Parent Session, n.d., 52).

The Influence of INSIGHTS on Children

Children are taught to expect problems as a part of life and learn to respond and not react to problems. They also learnt that everyone has problems. During a feedback session, a parent highlighted the influence the lesson had on her child's ability to resolve dilemmas. She shared that her six-year-old daughter witnessed a heated argument with her brother (the child's uncle). The child's immediate reaction was to try to placate the adults by stepping into their midst, and, with arms outstretched and pointing towards both parties, she said, "We have a dilemma." The adults were so shocked at the child's response that they stopped arguing and asked the child to repeat what she had said. The mother, a participant in the INSIGHTS programme at the time, explained to the uncle what a dilemma meant and what she and her child were learning at school. This intervention by this child brought an end to aggressive behaviours, which could have evolved into violence.

The INSIGHTS programme also emphasizes students' self-acceptance and acceptance of others. During every session, the students sing the following song:

> I'm unique (clap, clap). You're unique (clap, clap). We're all unique (clap, clap). And that's just fine. I'm unique (clap, clap). You're unique (clap, clap). We're all unique (clap, clap). And that's just fine. (What?) And that's just fine. (What?) And that's just fine (*INSIGHTS Manual*, Children Session. (INSIGHTS Manual, 6)

The Goodness of Fit theory that provides the foundation for understanding and training children based on their temperaments argues that the environment in which children develop must be conducive to their temperament. The environment is not necessarily physical but speaks to the psychological, social and emotional environment that parents and teachers create for nurturing children's development. Teachers are responsible for creating such an environment for children in the classroom and the school community. *The Diathesis-Stress Model* reinforces the importance of the environment in affecting children characteristics. Children with certain temperaments are likely to be more disposed to acting out severe problem behaviours in a stressful environment. The theory advocates that the environment should be as stress free as possible as children develop.

The empirical findings on the effects of INSIGHTS have implications for teachers and students' relationship in the classroom. Since the programme's implementation, there have been positive spin-offs manifested by less stress in the classroom, more time occupied in teaching and less time spent on managing students' behaviour. Overall, there has been improvement in the quality of the teacher-student relationship. The programme has also enhanced the parent-child relationship. Parents have become more accepting of their children and less frustrated and have additional time to build better relationships with their children. Early responses to children's negative behaviours have long-term effects if not managed well throughout their developmental stages. How children are trained from birth onwards directly affects their social and emotional development and determines the type of adults they become.

Conclusion

Childhood development is a process known to every adult. While there are three main areas of development – physical development, cognitive development, emotional and social development, the recognition and understanding of different temperaments among children focus on their emotional and social development. Emotional and social development addresses a child's competence to interact with others, including developing self-regulatory skills as the child matures. Children develop self-conscious emotions from infancy to toddlerhood, such as guilt, shame, embarrassment, envy and pride. These self-conscious emotions are potent in injuring or enhancing the child's sense of self (Berk 2014). Developing a balance in a child's self-conscious emotions requires adults' input from an early stage. For example, parents begin their tutoring very early in life when they say to the child, "Good boy [or good girl], look how far you threw that toy" or "Shame on you for grabbing that toy!" Acknowledging children's unique characteristics will instil in children, from early in their development, confidence and autonomy rather than "shame and doubt" (Berk 2014). Ultimately, children should be in an environment both at home and school where they can live as their true selves. Not in an environment where there is constant friction with who they are and how they express that self. Bullying and harsh discipline strategies rob children of their self-worth and confidence. Children should not develop in environments that cause an overwhelming fear of being perceived as different (Levine 2002). We, as adults, have a responsibility to help children enhance their strengths and manage their constraints. Interventions will help parents and teachers recognize children's temperaments, reframe how they view problem behaviours and respond rather than react to them.

Children can be traumatized by parents' behaviour, as noted earlier in chapter two. In addition, a parent's behaviour can traumatize a child early in their development through prolonged absence and neglect, domestic violence and sexual abuse (Miller and Howard 2022). This can lead the child to be aggressive and have maladjustment issues. The INSIGHTS programme does not target children who have been traumatized; instead, the programme focuses on enhancing the parent-child relationship and thus minimizing the likelihood of traumatic experiences in the home. On the issue of the effects of trauma on children's temperament, Paris (1998) concluded following an empirical investigation:

> Childhood trauma does not necessarily lead to adult personality disorders. Negative events are contributing factors to pathology, but not unique causes. The majority of children exposed to trauma are resilient. Children who are most resilient have adaptive personality traits, which increase the likelihood that they will form secure attachments and persist in their goals. They are also more likely to have had positive life experiences, which buffer the effects of stressful events. Some may even demonstrate "steeling," defined as increased adaptation as a result of negative experiences.
>
> These findings are in accord with the role of the "unshared environment" in adult personality and psychopathology. Taking into account the effects of genes does not mean downplaying the effects of childhood trauma. Rather, we need to develop methods to identify children who are particularly vulnerable to environmental insults. We need to explain the mechanisms that determine differences between children who are resilient and those who are not. (351)

Parents' and teachers' thinking and perception about their children and students' behaviour patterns influence their reactions to children and the nurturing environment they create for them (Martin, Lease and Slobodskaya 2020). For example, the teacher feels that a child is task persistent and attentive, but another child is emotionally difficult. Adults will interpret and respond to each child accordingly. The task persistent child will cause the teachers' job to be easier and less demanding, so teachers are more likely to be attentive. In contrast, the other child with emotional outbursts is more likely to solicit a negative response loaded with frustration.

Furthermore, how teachers and parents respond to the two types of behaviour is dependent on how they think about the child's reason(s) for the behaviours. Thus, adults' thinking and perception will influence the relationship between adults and children. Adults interacting with children must understand differences in children's behaviours and reactions to be effective guides and trainers. Self-reflection will bring self-awareness. These two components will help parents and teachers assess themselves and how their personalities add to the children's problem behaviour and how their stresses guide their interpretation of the children's behaviour. In other words, parents and teachers should be guided in examining their own emotions (McClowry 2014). A school must embrace the principle that every child has different educational needs.

References

Ainsworth, Mary D. Salter, Mary C. Blehar, and Sally C. Wall. 1978. *Patterns of Attachment: A Psychological Study of the Strange Situation*. New York: Lawrence Erlbaum Associates.

Allen, J. J., C.A. Anderson, and B.J. Bushman. 2018. "The General Aggression Model." *Current Opinion in Psychology* 19:75–80.

Archer, John. 1991a. "The Influence of Testosterone on Human Aggression." *British Journal of Psychology* 82 (1): 1–28. https://doi.org/10.1111/j.2044-8295.1991.tb02379.x.

Almas, Alisa N., Kathryn A. Degnan, Nathan A. Fox, Deborah A. Phillips, Heather A. Henderson, Olga Lydia Moas, and Amie Ashley Hane. 2011a. "The Relations between Infant Negative Reactivity, Non-Maternal Childcare, and Children's Interactions with Familiar and Unfamiliar Peers." *Social Development* 20 (4): 718–40. https://doi.org/10.1111/j.1467-9507.2011.00605.x.

Amos Clifford Center for Restorative Process (n.d.). Retrieved from https://www.healthiersf.org/RestorativePractices/ Resources/ documents/RP%20Curriculum%20and%20 Scripts%20 a n d%2 0 P oweP oin ts/ Classr oom %2 0 Cur r iculum / Teaching%20Restorative%20Practices%20 in%20the%20   Classroom%207%20lesson%20Curriculum. pdf.

Arseneault, Louise, Elizabeth J. Walsh, Kali H. Trzesniewski, Rhiannon Newcombe, Avshalom Caspi, and Terrie E. Moffitt. 2006. "Bullying Victimization Uniquely Contributes to Adjustment Problems in Young Children: A Nationally Representative Cohort Study." *Pediatrics* 118 (1): 130–38. https://doi.org/10.1542/peds.2005-2388.

Baker, Jean H. 2006. "Contributions of Teacher-Child Relationships to Positive School Adjustment during Elementary School." *Journal of School Psychology* 44 (3): 211–29. https://doi.org/10.1016/j.jsp.2006.02.002.

Baker, Jean H., Sycarah Grant, and Larissa Morlock. 2008. "The Teacher-Student Relationship as a Developmental Context for Children with Internalizing or Externalizing Behavior Problems." *School Psychology Quarterly* 23 (1): 3–15. https://doi.org/10.1037/1045-3830.23.1.3.

Bassett, Hideko Hamada, Susan A. Denham, Nicole B. Fettig, Timothy W. Curby, Man Mohtasham, and Nila Austin. 2017. "Temperament in the Classroom: Children Low in Surgency Are More Sensitive to Teachers' Reactions to Emotions." *International Journal of Behavioral Development* 41 (1): 4–14.

Baumrind, Diana. 1966. "Effects of Authoritative Parental Control of Child Behaviour." *Child Development* 37 (4): 887–907. http://arowe.pbworks.com/f/baumrind_1966_parenting.pdf.

Belsky, J. 1984. "The Determinants of Parenting: A Process Model." *Child Development* 55:83–96.

Berk, Laura E. 2014. *Development through the Lifespan*. Boston, MA: Allyn and Bacon.

Bernard Van Leer Foundation. (n.d.) https://bernardvanleer.org/about-us/.

Bertoni, Anna Marta Maria, Silvio Donato, Antonella Morgano, Raffaella Iafrate, and Rosa Rosnati. 2017. "A Qualitative Evaluation of a Preventive Intervention for Parents: The Groups for Family Enrichment Parent Version (GFE_P)." *Journal of Prevention and Intervention in the Community* 45 (3): 215–29. https://doi.org/10.1080/10852352.2016.1198135.

Blandon, Alysia Y., Susan D. Calkins, Susan P. Keane, and Marion O'Brien. 2010. "Contributions of Child's Physiology and Maternal Behavior to Children's Trajectories of Temperamental Reactivity." *Developmental Psychology* 46. (5): 1089–1102. https://doi.org/10.1037/a0020678.

Bowlby, John. 1988. "Developmental Psychiatry Comes of Age." The *American Journal of Psychiatry* 145 (1): 1–10. https://doi.org/10.1176/ajp.145.1.1.

Bronfenbrenner, Urie. 1974. *A Report on Longitudinal Evaluation of Preschool Programs*. https://files.eric.ed.gov/fulltext/ED093501.pdf

Brown, Janet, and Sharon Johnson. 2008. "Childrearing and Child Participation in Jamaican Families." *International Journal of Early Years Education* 16 (1): 31–40. https://doi.org/10.1080/09669760801892110.

Burke, Taniesha, and Leon Kuczynski. 2018. "Jamaican Mothers' Perceptions of Children's Strategies for Resisting Parental Rules and Requests." *Frontiers in Psychology* 9:1786. doi: 10.3389/fpsyg.2018.01786.

Campbell, S. 1979. "Mother-infant Interaction as a Function of Maternal Ratings of Temperament." *Child Psychiatry and Human Development* 10:67–76.

Caribbean Policy Research Institute. 2012. *2012 Report Card on Education in Jamaica.* https://docs.google.com/viewerng/viewer?url=https://www.capricaribbean.org/sites/default/files/public/documents/report/2012_report_card_on_education_in_jamaica.pdf.

Carlson, Elizabeth. 1998. "A Prospective Longitudinal Study of Attachment Disorganization/Disorientation." *Child Development* 68 (4): 1107–1128.

Caspi, A., and P.A. Silva. 1995. "Temperamental Qualities at Age Three Predict Personality Traits in Young Adults: Longitudinal Evidence from a Birth Cohort." *Child Development* 66:486–98. https://doi.org/10.2307/1131592.

Cassidy, Jude, Steven J. Kirsh, Krista L. Scolton, and Ross D. Parke. 1996. "Attachment and Representations of Peer Relationships." *Developmental Psychology* 32 (5): 892–904. https://doi.org/10.1037/0012-1649.32.5.892.

Chao, Ruth K. 2001. "Extending Research on the Consequences of Parenting Style for Chinese Americans and European Americans." *Child Development* 72 (6): 1832–43.

Chapell, Mark S., Stefanie L. Hasselman, Theresa Kitchin, Safiya N. Lomon, Kenneth W. MacIver, and Patrick L. Sarullo. 2006. "Bullying in Elementary School, High School, and College." *Adolescence* 41 (164): 633–48.

Cappella, Elise, Erin E. O'Connor, Megan P. McCormick, Ashley R. Turbeville, Ashleigh J. Collins, and Sandee G. McClowry. 2015. "Class Wide Efficacy of INSIGHTS: Observed Student Behaviors and Teacher Practices in Kindergarten and First Grade." *Elementary School Journal* 116 (2): 217–41. https://doi.org/10.1086/683983.

Chamundeswari, S. 2013. "Teacher Management Styles and Their Influence on Performance and Leadership Development among Students at the Secondary Level." *International*

Journal of Academic Research in Progressive Education and Development 2 (1): 367–418.

Clunies-Ross, Phil, Emma Little, and Mandy Kienhuis. 2008. "Self-reported and Actual Use of Proactive and Reactive Classroom Management Strategies and Their Relationship with Teacher Stress and Student Behaviour." *Educational Psychology* 28 (6): 693–710. https://doi.org/10.1080/01443410802206700.

Collins, Asleigh, and Sandee McClowry. 2012. "Temperament-Based Intervention: Reconceptualized from a Response-to-Intervention Framework." *Handbook of Temperament*, January, 607–27. https://dialnet.unirioja.es/servlet/articulo?codigo=7848258.

Collins, W. Andrew, Eleanor E. Maccoby, Laurence Steinberg, E. Mavis Hetherington, and Marc H. Bornstein. 2000. "Contemporary Research on Parenting: The Case for Nature and Nurture." *American Psychologist* 55 (2): 218–32. https://doi.org/10.1037/0003-066x.55.2.218.

Cook, Loraine D., and Garth Lipps. 2020. "An Examination of a Temperament-Based Intervention in Selected Early Childhood Institutions in Jamaica." *Journal of Development Effectiveness* 12 (1): 1–13. https://doi.org/10.1080/19439342.2020.1724177.

Coplan, Robert J., Kathleen Hughes, Sandra Bosacki, and Linda Rose-Krasnor. 2011a. "Is Silence Golden? Elementary School Teachers' Strategies and Beliefs Regarding Hypothetical Shy/Quiet and Exuberant/Talkative Children." *Journal of Educational Psychology* 103 (4): 939–51. https://doi.org/10.1037/a0024551.

Coplan, Robert J., and Kavita Prakash. 2003. "Spending Time with Teacher: Characteristics of Preschoolers Who Frequently Elicit versus Initiate Interactions with Teachers." *Early Childhood Research Quarterly* 18 (1): 143–58. https://doi.org/10.1016/s0885-2006(03)00009-7.

Coplan, Robert J., and K.H. Rubin. 2010. "Social Withdrawal and Shyness in Childhood: History, Theories, Definitions and Assessments." In *The Development of Shyness and Social Withdrawal*, edited by Kenneth H. Rubin and Robert J. Coplan, 42–63. New York, NY: Guilford Press.

Crozier, W. R. 2010. "Shyness and the Development of Embarrassment and the Self-Conscious Emotions." In *The Development of Shyness and Social Withdrawal*, edited by Kenneth H. Rubin and Robert J. Coplan, 42–63. New York, NY: Guilford Press.

Curby, Timothy W., Kathleen Moritz Rudasill, Taylor Edwards, and Koraly Pérez-Edgar. 2011. "The Role of Classroom Quality in

Ameliorating the Academic and Social Risks Associated with Difficult Temperament." *School Psychology Quarterly* 26 (2): 175–88. https://doi.org/10.1037/a0023042.

Deater-Deckard, Kirby, and Zhe Wang. 2012. "Development of Temperament and Attention: Behavioral Genetic Approaches." In *Cognitive Neuroscience of Attention*, 2nd ed., edited by M.I. Posner, 331–42. NY: The Guilford Press.

Delker, Brianna C., Rosemary E. Bernstein, and Heidimarie R. Laurent. 2018. "Out of Harm's Way: Secure versus Insecure – Disorganized Attachment Predicts Less Adolescent Risk-taking Related to Childhood Poverty." *Development and Psychopathology* 30:283–96.

Demeusy, Elizabeth M., Elizabeth D. Handley, Fred A. Rogosch, Dante Cicchetti, and Sheree L. Toth. 2018. "Early Neglect and the Development of Aggression in Toddlerhood: The Role of Working Memory." *Child Maltreatment*, June 23 (4): 344–54. https://doi.org/10.1177/1077559518778814.

Dollar, Jessica M., Nicole B. Perry, Susan D. Calkins, Susan P. Keane, and Lilly Shanahan. 2018. "Temperamental Anger and Positive Reactivity and the Development of Social Skills: Implications for Academic Competence During Preadolescence." *Early Education and Development* 29 (5): 747–61. https://doi.org/10.1080/10409289.2017.1409606.

Doumen, Sarah, Karin Verschueren, Evelien Buyse, Veerle Germeijs, Koen Luyckx, and Bart Soenens. 2008. "Reciprocal Relations between Teacher-Child Conflict and Aggressive Behavior in Kindergarten: A Three-wave Longitudinal Study." *Journal of Clinical Child and Adolescent Psychology* 37 (3): 588–99.

Dudley Ransford Brandyce Grant (1915–1988). https://publications.iadb.org/bitstream/handle/11319/7773/Crime-and-Violence-in-Jamaica-IDB-Series-on-Crime-and-Violence-in-the-Caribbean.pdf?sequence=4.

Fernald, Lia C., and Julie Meeks-Gardner. 2003. "Jamaican Children's Reports of Violence at School and Home." *Social and Economic Studies* 52 (4): 121–40.

Fox, Nathan A., Heather A. Henderson, Koraly Pérez-Edgar, and Lauren K. White. 2008. "The Biology of Temperament: An Integrative Approach." In *The MIT Press EBooks*. https://doi.org/10.7551/mitpress/7437.003.0060.

Garcia, Fernando, and Enrique Gracia. 2009. "Is Always Authoritative the Optimum Parenting Style? Evidence from Spanish Families." *PubMed* 44 (173): 101–31. https://pubmed.ncbi.nlm.nih.gov/19435170.

Gilède, Roberto Posada. 2012. "Experiences of Violence and Moral Reasoning in a Context of Vengeance." *Revista Colombiana De Psicología* 21 (2): 197–212. https://dialnet.unirioja.es/descarga/articulo/4287000.pdf.

Gallagher, Emily. 2014. "Teacher-student Conflict and Student Aggression in Kindergarten." https://steinhardt.nyu.edu/appsych/opus/issues/2014/spring/gallagher.

Goldsmith, H. Hill, and Catherine Harman. 1994. "Temperament and Attachment: Individuals and Relationships." *Current Directions in Psychological Science* 3 (2): 53–57. https://doi.org/10.1111/1467-8721.ep10769948.

Goodman, G., R.C. Bartlett, and Martha Stroh. 2013. "Mothers' Borderline Features and Children's Disorganized Attachment Representations as Predictors of Children's Externalizing Behaviours." *Psychoanalytic Psychology* 30 (1): 16–36.

Greenberg, M. T., M. Speltz, and M. DeKlyen. 1993. "The Role of Attachment in the Early Development of Disruptive Behaviour Problems." *Development and Psychopathology* 5:191–213. doi:10.1017/S095457940000434X.

Grusec, Joan E., Maayan Davidov, and Leah Lundell. 2002. "Prosocial and Helping Behavior." In *Blackwell's Handbook of Childhood Social Development*, edited by Peter K. Smith Craig H. Hart 457–72. Malden, MA: Blackwell.

Guerra, Nancy G., L. Rowell Huesmann, and Anja Spindler. 2003. "Community Violence Exposure, Social Cognition, and Aggression among Urban Elementary School Children." *Child Development* 74 (5): 1561–76. https://doi.org/10.1111/1467-8624.00623.

Hamby, Sherry, and John H. Grych. 2012. *The Web of Violence: Exploring Connections among Different Forms of Interpersonal Violence and Abuse*. https://epublications.marquette.edu/marq_fac-book/112/.

Hamre, Bridget K., and Robert C. Pianta. 2001. "Early Teacher-Child Relationships and the Trajectory of Children's School Outcomes Through Eighth Grade." *Child Development* 72 (2): 625–38. http://www.jstor.org/stable/1132418.

Han, Changsu, Yong Jin Kim, Myung-Jin Choi, Ji Sang Hyun, Yun Shik Choi, and Min Goo Lee. 2004. "Serotonergic Genes and Personality Traits in the Korean Population." *Neuroscience Letters* 354 (1): 2–5. https://doi.org/10.1016/s0304-3940(03)00753-5.

Harrison, Judith A., Kimberly J. Vannest, John M. Davis, and Cecil R. Reynolds. 2012. "Common Problem Behaviors of Children and Adolescents in General Education Classrooms in the United

States." *Journal of Emotional and Behavioral Disorders* 20 (1): 55–64. https://doi.org/10.1177/1063426611421157.

Hart, Craig H., Lloyd Newell, and Susanne Frost Olsen. 2008. "Parenting Skills and Social-Communicative Competence in Childhood." In *Handbook of Communication and Social Interaction Skills*, edited by John O. Greene and Brant R. Burleson, 753–97. Mahwah, NJ: Lawrence Erlbaum Associates.

Hartup, Willard W., and Shirley M. Moore. 1990. "Early Peer Relations: Developmental Significance and Prognostic Implications." *Early Childhood Research Quarterly* 5 (1): 1–17. https://doi.org/10.1016/0885-2006(90)90002-i.

Harriott, Anthony D., and Marlyn Jones. 2016. *Crime and Violence in Jamaica*. Kingston, Jamaica: Inter- American Development Bank. Retrieved from: https://publications.iadb.org/en/publication/12510/crime-and-violence-jamaica-idb-series-crime-and-violence-caribbean.

Henningham-Baker, H., J. Meeks-Gardner, S. Chang, and Walker, S. 2009. "Experiences of Violence and Deficits in Academic Achievement among Urban Primary School Children in Jamaica." *Child Abuse and Neglect* 33:296–306.

Hipson, Will E., and Daniel G. Séguin. 2016. "Is Good Fit Related to Good Behaviour? Goodness of Fit between Daycare Teacher-Child Relationships, Temperament, and Prosocial Behaviour." *Early Child Development and Care* 186 (5): 785–98. https://doi.org/10.1080/03004430.2015.1061518.

Hong, Yoo Jin, and Jae Yong Park. 2012. "Impact of Attachment, Temperament and Parenting on Human Development." *Korean Journal of Pediatrics* 55 (12): 449. https://doi.org/10.3345/kjp.2012.55.12.449.

Howes, C., and C.C. Matheson. 1992. "Sequences in the Development of Competent Play with Peers: Social and Social Pretend Play." *Developmental Psychology* 28 (5): 961–974. INSIGHTS Manual.

Howes, Carollee, Claire Hamilton, and Catherine Matheson. 1994. "Children's Relationships with Peers: Differential Associations with Aspects of the Teacher-Child Relationship." *Child Development* 65 (1): 253–63. https://doi.org/10.2307/1131379.

Jones, Vernon. F., and Louise S. Jones. 2015. *Comprehensive Classroom Management: Creating Communities of Support and Solving Problems*. London: Pearson.

Kagan, Jerome, and Nancy Snidman. 2004. *The Long Shadow of Temperament*. Cambridge, MA: The Belknap Press of Harvard University Press.

Keogh, B. 2003. *Temperament in the Classroom: Understanding Individual Differences.* Baltimore, MD: Paul H. Brookes Publishing Co. "Is temperament determined by genetics?" (n.d.). https://medlineplus. gov/genetics/understanding/traits/temperament/.

Knutson, John F., David S. DeGarmo, Gina Koeppl, and John L. Reid. 2005. "Care Neglect, Supervisory Neglect, and Harsh Parenting in the Development of Children's Aggression: A Replication and Extension." *Child Maltreatment* 10 (2): 92–107. https://doi.org/10.1177/1077559504273684.

Koenen, Anne-Katrien, Eleonora Vervoort, Geert Kelchtermans, Karine Verschueren, and Jantine L. Spilt. 2019. "Teachers' Daily Negative Emotions in Interactions with Individual Students in Special Education." *Journal of Emotional and Behavioral Disorders* 27 (1): 37–51. https://doi.org/10.1177/1063426617739579.

Kornienko, Dimitry S. 2016. "Child Temperament and Mother's Personality as a Predictor of Maternal Relation to Child". *Social and Behavioral Sciences* 233:343–47.

Kotch, Jonathan B., Terri L. Lewis, Jon M. Hussey, Diana J. English, Ricardo Thompson, Alan J. Litrownik, Desmond K. Runyan, Shrikant I. Bangdiwala, Benjamin Margolis, and Howard Dubowitz. 2008. "Importance of Early Neglect for Childhood Aggression." *Pediatrics* 121 (4): 725–31. https://doi.org/10.1542/peds.2006-3622.

Ladd, G.W., and G.S. Pettit. 2002. "Parenting and the Development of Children's Peer Relationships." In *Handbook of Parenting: Practical Issues in Parenting*, edited by Marc H. Bornstein, 269–309. Mahwah, NJ: Lawrence Erlbaum Associates.

Lamb, Michael E. 1977a. "Father-Infant and Mother-Infant Interaction in the First Year of Life." *Child Development* 48 (1): 167. https://doi.org/10.2307/1128896.

———. 1977b. "The Development of Mother-Infant and Father-Infant Attachments in the Second Year of Life." *Developmental Psychology* 13 (6): 637–48. https://doi.org/10.1037/0012-1649.13.6.637.

———. 2010. "How Do Fathers Influence Children's Development? Let Me Count the Ways." In The *Role of the Father in Child Development* edited by Michael E. Lamb, 1–26. Hoboken, NJ: John Wiley and Sons.

Lyons-Ruth, K. 1996. "Attachment Relationships among Children with Aggressive Behaviour Problems: The Role of Disorganized Early Attachment Patterns." *Journal of Consulting and Clinical Psychology*, Feb 64 (1): 64–73.

Laukkanen, Johanna, Ulriika Ojansuu, Asko Tolvanen, Saija Alatupa, and Kaisa Aunola. 2014. "Child's Difficult Temperament and Mothers' Parenting Styles." *Journal of Child and Family Studies* 23 (2): 312–23. https://doi.org/10.1007/s10826-013-9747-9.

Levine, M. 2002. *A Mind at a Time*. London: Simon and Schuster.

Main, M., and Solomon, J. 1986. "Discovery of an Insecure-Disorganized/Disoriented Attachment Pattern." In *Affective Development in Infancy*, edited by T. Berry Brazelton and Michael W. Yogman, 95–124. Westport, CT: Ablex.

Marcus, Robert F. 2017. *The Development of Aggression and Violence in Adolescence*. New York, NY: Palgrave Macmillan.

Martin, Anne, Rebecca Ryan, and Jeanne Brooks-Gunn. 2013. "Longitudinal Associations among Interest, Persistence, Supportive Parenting, and Achievement in Early Childhood." *Early Childhood Research Quarterly* 28 (4): 658–67. https://doi.org/10.1016/j.ecresq.2013.05.003.

Martin, Roy P., A. Michele Lease, and Helena R. Slobodskaya. 2020. *Temperament and Children: Profiles of Individual Differences*. Springer. https://doi.org/10.1007/978-3-030-62208-4.

Martin, Roy P. 1994. "Child Temperament and Common Problems in Schooling: Hypotheses about Causal Connections." *Journal of School Psychology* 32 (2): 119–34. https://doi.org/10.1016/0022-4405(94)90006-x.

Martin, R. P., and J. Holbrook. 1985. "Relationship of Temperament Characteristics to the Academic Achievement of First-Grade Children." *Journal of Psychoeducational Assessment* 3 (2): 131–40. https://doi.org/10.1177/073428298500300204.

Masten, Ann S., Glenn I. Roisman, Jeffrey R. Long, Keith B. Burt, Jelena Obradović, Jennifer Riley, Kristen Boelcke-Stennes, and Auke Tellegen. 2005. "Developmental Cascades: Linking Academic Achievement and Externalizing and Internalizing Symptoms Over 20 Years." *Developmental Psychology* 41 (5): 733–46. https://doi.org/10.1037/0012-1649.41.5.733.

McClowry, S. (n.d.). *INSIGHTS into Children's Temperament Manual*. New York: New York University.

McClowry Graham, Sandee. 2014. *Temperament-Based Elementary Classroom Management*. Lanham, Maryland: Rowman and Littlefield.

McClowry, Sandee, and Mark Spellman. 2016. "Assessing the Cultural Relevance of INSIGHTS for Jamaica." *Caribbean Journal of Education* 38 (1): 73–93.

McClowry, Sandra Graham, Eileen T. Rodriguez, Catherine S. Tamis-LeMonda, Mark E Spellmann, Allyson Carlson and David L. Snow. 2013. "Teacher/Student Interactions and Classroom Behavior: The Role of Student Temperament and Gender." *Journal of Research in Childhood Education* 27 (3): 283–301.

McClowry, S. Graham, R.L. Hegvik, and H. Teglasi. 1993. "An Examination of the Construct Validity of the Middle Childhood Temperament Questionnaire." *Merrill-Palmer Quarterly* 39 (2): 279-293.

McClowry, Sandee G., and Ashleigh Collins, 2012. "Temperament-Based Intervention: Reconceptualized from a Response- to-Intervention Framework." In *Handbook of Temperament*, edited by Marcel Zentner and Rebecca L. Shiner, 581–603. New York, NY: Guilford Press.

McClowry, Sandra Graham, David A. Snow, Catherine S. Tamis-LeMonda, and Eileen T. Rodriguez. 2010. "Testing the Efficacy of INSIGHTS on Student Disruptive Behavior, Classroom Management, and Student Competence in Inner City Primary Grades." *School Mental Health*, March. https://doi.org/10.1007/s12310-009-9023-8.

McCormick, Meghan P., Elizabeth O'Connor, Elise Cappella, and Sandee McClowry. 2015. "Getting a Good Start in School: Effects of INSIGHTS on Children with High Maintenance Temperaments." *Early Childhood Research Quarterly* 30 (January): 128–39. https://doi.org/10.1016/j.ecresq.2014.10.006.

Meehan, Barbara T., Jan N. Hughes, and Timothy A. Cavell. 2003. "Teacher-Student Relationships as Compensatory Resources for Aggressive Children." *Child Development* 74 (4): 1145–57. https://doi.org/10.1111/1467-8624.00598.

McKenzie, Melissa D., and Robert B. Casselman. 2017. "Perceived Father Rejection and Young Adult Aggression: Examining Mediational Components of Emotional Dysregulation." *Journal of Family Issues* 38 (8):1089–1108.

Meeks-Gardner, Julie, Christine Powell, Joan Thomas and Doreen Millard. 2003. "Perceptions and Experiences of Violence among Secondary School Students in Urban Jamaica." *Pan American Journal of Public Health* 14:97–103.

Mervielde, Ivan, and Sarah S.W. De Pauw. 2012. "Models of Child Temperament." In *Handbook of Temperament*, edited by Marcel Zentner and Rebecca L. Shiner, 21–40. New York, NY: Guilford Press.

Miller, Carol, and Jamie J. Howard. 2022. "How Trauma Affects Kids in School." https://childmind.org/article/how-trauma-affects-kids-school.

Mokrova, Irina, Marion O'Brien, Susan D. Calkins, Esther M. Leerkes and Stuart Marcovitch, S. 2013. "The Role of Persistence at Preschool Age in Academic Skills at Kindergarten." *European Journal of Psychology of Education* 28 (4): 1495–503. doi: 10.1007/s10212-013-0177-2.

Moretti, M. M., and Peled, M. 2004. "Adolescent-Parent Attachment: Bonds that Support Healthy Development." *Pediatrics and Child Health* 9 (8): 551–55.

Moore, Sophie E., Rosana E. Norman, Peter D. Sly, Andrew J. O. Whitehouse, Stephen R. Zubrick, and James Scott. 2014. "Adolescent Peer Aggression and Its Association with Mental Health and Substance Use in an Australian Cohort." *Journal of Adolescence* 37 (1): 11–21. https://doi.org/10.1016/j.adolescence.2013.10.006.

Moretti, Marlene M., and Maya Peled. 2004. "Adolescent-Parent Attachment: Bonds That Support Healthy Development." *Paediatrics and Child Health* 9 (8): 551–55. https://doi.org/10.1093/pch/9.8.551.

National Library of Jamaica (n.d). Dudley Ransford Brandyee Grant (1915–1988). https://nlj.gov.jm/biographies/dudley-ransford-brandyee-grant-1915-1988/

Nelson, J. Ron, and Maura L. 2000. "Ongoing Reciprocal Teacher-Student Interactions Involving Disruptive Behaviours in General Education Classrooms." *Journal of Emotional and Behavioural Disorders* 8 (1): 27–48.

O'Connor, Elizabeth, Eric Dearing, and Brian T. Collins. 2012. "Teacher-Child Relationship and Behavior Problem Trajectories in Elementary School." *American Educational Research Journal* 48 (1): 120–62. https://doi.org/10.3102/0002831210365008.

O'Connor, Elizabeth, Marc Scott, Meghan P. McCormick, and Sharon L. Weinberg. 2014. "Early Mother-Child Attachment and Behavior Problems in Middle Childhood: The Role of the Subsequent Caregiving Environment." *Attachment and Human Development* 16 (6): 590–612. https://doi.org/10.1080/14616734.2014.937817.

O'Connor, Erin E., Elise Cappella, Meghan P. McCormick, and Sandee McClowry. 2014. "Enhancing the Academic Development of Shy Children: A Test of the Efficacy of INSIGHTS." *School Psychology Review* 43 (3): 239–59. https://doi.org/10.1080/02796015.2014.12087426.

O'Connor, E.E., M.A. Scott, M.P. McCormick, and S.L. Weinberg, 2014. "Early Mother-Child Attachment and Behavior Problems in

Middle Childhood: The Role of the Subsequent Caregiving Environment." *Attachment and Human Development* 16 (6): 590–612. http://dx.doi.org/10.1080/14616734.2014.937817.

Oren, Meral, and Ithel Jones. 2009. "The Relationships between Child Temperament, Teacher-Child Relationships, and Teacher-Child Interactions." *International Education Studies* 2 (4): 122–31. https://doi.org/10.5539/ies.v2n4p122.

Őneren Şendil, Çağla 2010. "An Investigation of Social Competence and Behavioural Problems of 5–6 Year – Old Children Through Peer Preference, Temperament and Gender." Master of Science Thesis, Middle East Technical University. https://open.metu.edu.tr/handle/11511/20333.

Palisin, Helen E. 1986. "Preschool Temperament and Performance on Achievement Tests." *Developmental Psychology* 22 (6): 766–70. https://doi.org/10.1037/0012-1649.22.6.766.

Pallini, Susanna, Roberto Baiocco, Barry I. Schneider, Sheri Madigan, and Leslie Atkinson. 2014. "Early Child–Parent Attachment and Peer Relations: A Meta-Analysis of Recent Research." *Journal of Family Psychology* 28 (1): 118–23. https://doi.org/10.1037/a0035736.

Paris, Joel. 1998. "Does Childhood Trauma Cause Personality Disorders in Adults?" *The Canadian Journal of Psychiatry* 43 (2): 148–53. https://doi.org/10.1177/070674379804300203.

Parke, R., McDowell, D., Kim, M., Killan, C., Dennis, J., Flyr, M. L., and Wild, M. 2002. "Fathers' Contributions to Children's Peer Relationships." In *Handbook of Father Involvement: Multidisciplinary Perspectives*, edited by Catherine S. Tamis-Lemonda, 141–167. Mahway, NJ: Lawrence Erlbaum Associates.

Parker, Jeffrey B., and Steven R. Asher. 1987. "Peer Relations and Later Personal Adjustment: Are Low-Accepted Children at Risk?" *Psychological Bulletin* 102 (3): 357–89. https://doi.org/10.1037/0033-2909.102.3.357.

Parker, Jeffrey G., Kenneth H. Rubin, Stephen A. Erath, Julie C. Wojslawowicz, Allison A. Buskirk. 2006. "Peer Relationships, Child Development, and Adjustment: A Developmental Psycho-Pathological Perspective." In *Developmental Psychopathology: Theory and Methods*, edited by Dante Cicchetti and Donald Cohen, 419–93. Hoboken, NJ: John Wiley and Sons.

Pasco Fearon, R.M., and Jay Belsky. 2011. "Infant-mother Attachment and the Growth of Externalizing Problems across the Primary-School Years." *Journal of Child Psychology and Psychiatry* 52 (7): 782–91.

Pekdoğan, Serpil, and Mehmet Kanak. 2016. "A Study on Social Competence and Temperament of Pre-School Children's." *Journal of Education and Learning*, September. https://doi.org/10.5539/jel.v5n4p133.

Pianta, Robert C. 1997. "Adult-Child Relationship Processes and Early Schooling." *Early Education and Development* 8 (1): 11–26. https://doi.org/10.1207/s15566935eed0801_2.

Piquero, Alex R., David P. Farrington, Brandon C. Welsh, Richard E. Tremblay, and Wesley G. Jennings. 2009. "Effects of Early Family/Parent Training Programs on Antisocial Behavior and Delinquency." *Journal of Experimental Criminology* 5 (2): 83–120. https://doi.org/10.1007/s11292-009-9072-x.

Planalp, Elizabeth M., and M. Julia. Braungart-Rieker. 2013. "Temperamental Precursors of Infant Attachment with Mothers and Fathers." *Infant Behavior and Development* 36:796–808.

Plomin, R. 2018. *Blueprint: How DNA Makes Us Who We Are*. New York, NY: Penguin.

Pottinger, A., and K. Nelson. 2004. "A Climate of Punishment in Jamaican Classrooms: Attitudes, Beliefs and Use of Disciplinary Practices by Educators." *Caribbean Journal of Psychology* 1:22–38.

Pruett, Marsha Kline, Lauren E. Arthur, and Rachel Ebling. 2007. "The Hand That Rocks the Cradle: Maternal Gatekeeping after Divorce." *Pace Law Review* 27 (4): 709. https://doi.org/10.58948/2331-3528.1139.

Reebye, P. 2005. "Aggression During Early Years – Infancy and Preschool." *The Canadian Child and Adolescent Psychiatry Review* 14 (1): 16–20.

Rochat, Philippe. 2003. "Five Levels of Self-awareness as They Unfold Early in Life." *Consciousness and Cognition* 12:717–31.

Rose-Krasnor, Linda, Kenneth H. Rubin, Cathryn L. Booth, and Robert J. Coplan. 1996. "The Relation of Maternal Directiveness and Child Attachment Security to Social Competence in Preschoolers." *International Journal of Behavioral Development*, June. https://doi.org/10.1177/016502549601900205.

Rothbart, Mary K. 2007. "Temperament, Development, and Personality." *Current Directions in Psychological Science* 16 (4): 207–12. https://doi.org/10.1111/j.1467-8721.2007.00505.x.

Rothbart, M.K. 2012. "Advances in temperament: History, Concepts, and Measures." In *Handbook of Temperament,* edited by

Marc Zentner and Rebecca L. Shiner, 3–20. New York, NY: Guilford Press.

Rothbart, Mary K., and John E. Bates. 2006. "Temperament." In *Handbook of Child Psychology: Social, Emotional, and Personality Development, Volume 6th edition*, edited by Nancy Eisenberg, Willam Damon and Richard Lerner, 99–166. New York, NY: John Wiley and Sons.

Rubin, Kenneth. H., Julie C. Bowker, and H. Gazelle. 2010. "Social Withdrawal in Childhood and Adolescence: Peer Relationships and Social Competence". In *The Development of Shyness and Social Withdrawal*, edited by Robert J. Coplan and Kenneth H. Rubin, 131–55. New York, NY: Guilford Press.

Rudasill, Kathleen Moritz. 2011. "Child Temperament, Teacher-Child Interactions, and Teacher-Child Relationships: A Longitudinal Investigation from First to Third Grade." *Early Childhood Research Quarterly* 26 (2): 147–56. https://doi.org/10.1016/j.ecresq.2010.07.002.

———, Kathleen Gallagher, and Jamie White. 2010. "Temperamental Attention and Activity, Classroom Emotional Support, and Academic Achievement in Third Grade." *Journal of School Psychology* 48 (2): 113–34. https://doi.org/10.1016/j.jsp.2009.11.002.

Runions, None Kevin C., None Frank Vitaro, None Donna Cross, and None Georges Boivin. 2014. "Teacher-Child Relationship, Parenting, and Growth in Likelihood and Severity of Physical Aggression in the Early School Years." *Merrill-Palmer Quarterly-Journal of Developmental Psychology* 60 (3): 274. https://doi.org/10.13110/merrpalmquar1982.60.3.0274.

Saal, Frederick S. Vom. 1983. "Models of Early Hormonal Effects on Intrasex Aggression in Mice." In *Springer EBooks*, 197–222. https://doi.org/10.1007/978-1-4613-3521-4_9.

Samms-Vaughan, M.E., M.A. Jackson, M.A., and D.E. Ashley. 2005. "Urban Jamaican Children's Exposure to Community Violence." *West Indian Medical Journal* 54:14–21.

Schneider, Barry Howard, Leslie Richard Atkinson and Christine Tardif. 2001. "Child-Parent Attachment and Children's Peer Relations: A Quantitative Review." *Developmental Psychology* 37 (1): 86–100.

Serrbanescu, Florina, Alicia Ruiz, and Danielle Suchdev. 2010. *Reproductive Health Survey 2008*. Kingston, Jamaica: National Family Planning Board. https://jnfpb.org/wp-content/uploads/2019/11/2008-RHS-Final-Report.pdf.

Sheridan, Susan M., Carolyn Pope Edwards, Christine A. Marvin, and Lisa L. Knoche. 2009. "Professional Development in Early Childhood Programs: Process Issues and Research Needs." *Early Education and Development* 20 (3): 377–401.

Smiley, Patricia A., Sherylle J. Tan, Alison Goldstein, and Jennifer Sweda. 2016. "Mother Emotion, Child Temperament, and Young Children's Helpless Responses to Failure." *Social Development*, 25 (2): 285–303.

Stams, Geert Jan J.M., Femmie Juffer, and Marinus H. Van IJzendoorn. 2002. "Maternal Sensitivity, Infant Attachment, and Temperament in Early Childhood Predict Adjustment in Middle Childhood: The Case of Adopted Children and Their Biologically Unrelated Parents." *Developmental Psychology* 38 (5): 806–21. https://doi.org/10.1037/0012-1649.38.5.806.

Storey, Kim, and Ron Slaby. 2013. "Eyes on Bullying in Early Childhood." Education Development Center. http://www.pr om otepr ev en t. or g/ si tes/ www. promoteprevent.org/files/resources/Eyes%20on%20 Bullying%20in%20Early%20Childhood_1.pdf.

Solomon, Judith, and Carol George. 2011. "The Disorganized Attachment-Caregiving System: Dysregulation of Adaptive Processes at Multiple Levels." In *Disorganized Attachment and Caregiving*, edited by Judith Solomon and Carol George, 3–24. New York, NY: Guilford Press.

Sullivan-Choppe, Sarah J., Geoffrey L. Brown, Elizabeth A. Cannon, Sarah C. Mangelsdorf, and Margaret Sokolowski-Szewezyk. 2008. "Maternal Gatekeeping, Co-Parenting Quality, and Fathering Behavior in Families with Infants." *Journal of Family Psychology* 22 (3): 389–98.

Tharner, Anne, Maartje P.C.M. Luijk, Marinus H. Van IJzendoorn, Marian J. Bakermans-Kranenburg, Vincent W. V. Jaddoe, Albert Hofman, Frank C. Verhulst, and Henning Tiemeier. 2012. "Infant Attachment, Parenting Stress, and Child Emotional and Behavioral Problems at Age 3 Years." *Parenting Science* 12 (4): 261–81. https://doi.org/10.1080/15295192.2012.709150.

The Jamaican Reproductive Survey 2008. 2010. http://jnfpb.org/assets/2008%20RHS%20Young%20Adults%20Report.pdf.

———. 2010. http://jnfpb.org/assets/2008%20Final%20Report%20Jamaica.pdf.

Thomas, Alexander, and Stella Chess. 1977. *Temperament and Development*. New York, NY: Brunner/Mazel.

Thomas, Alexander, Stella Chess, Herbert G. Birch, Margaret Hertzig and Sam Korn. 1964. *Behavioural Individuality in Early Childhood*. New York: New York University Press.
Thomas, Duane E., Karen L. Bierman, and Christopher J. Powers. 2011. "The Influence of Classroom Aggression and Classroom Climate on Aggressive-Disruptive Behavior." *Child Development* 82 (3): 751–57. https://doi.org/10.1111/j.1467-8624.2011.01586.x.
Thomas, Duane E., Karen L. Bierman, Celine I. Thompson, and Christopher J. Powers. 2008. "Double Jeopardy: Child and School Characteristics That Predict Aggressive-Disruptive Behavior in First Grade." *School Psychology Review* 37 (4): 516–32. https://doi.org/10.1080/02796015.2008.12087865.
Tremblay, R.E. "The Development and Prevention of Physical Aggression." In *Encyclopedia on Early Childhood Development*, topic edited by R.E. Tremblay M. Boivin, and R. Dev Peters, [online]. https://www.child-encyclopedia.com/aggression/according-experts/development-and-prevention-physical-aggression.
———., J. Gervais, and A. Petitclerc. 2008. *Early Childhood Learning Prevents Youth Violence*. Montreal, Quebec: Centre of Excellence for Early Childhood Development.
van den Boom, Dymphna C. 1994. "The Influence of Temperament and Mothering on Attachment and Exploration: An Experimental Manipulation of Sensitive Responsiveness among Lower-Class Mothers with Irritable Infants." *Child Development* 65 (5): 1457–77. https://doi.org/10.2307/1131511.
van der Veer, René. 2007. *Lev Vygotsky*. London: Continuing International Publishing.
Webster-Stratton, Carolyn, and Keith C. Herman. 2010. "Disseminating Incredible Years Series Early-Intervention Programs: Integrating and Sustaining Services between School and Home." *Psychology in the Schools* 47 (1): 36–54. https://doi.org/10.1002/pits.20450.
Wong, M. 2017. "Chinese Children's Perceptions of Aggression among Peers at School." *Early Years* 37 (2): 143–157. doi: 10.1080/09575146.2016.1178711.
A World Bank Report. (n.d.). *Jamaica: The Challenge of Social Service Provision in the Political Arena*. http://siteresources.worldbank.org/EXTSOCIALDEV/Resources/3177394-1168615404141/3328201-1192042053459/Jamaica.pdf?resourceurlname=Jamaica.pdf.
Yaros, Anna, John E. Lochman, and Karen C. Wells. 2016. "Parental Aggression as a Predictor of Boys' Hostile Attribution across

the Transition to Middle School." *International Journal of Behavioral Development* 40 (5): 452–58. https://doi.org/10.1177/0165025415607085.

Ybrandt, Helene, and Kerstin Armelius. 2010. "Peer Aggression and Mental Health Problems: Self-Esteem as a Mediator." *School Psychology International* 31 (2): 146–63.

Yoleri, Sibel. 2016. "Teacher-Child Relationships in Preschool Period: The Roles of Child Temperament and Language Skills." *International Electronic Journal of Elementary Education* 9 (1): 210–24.

Zuckerman, M. 2012. "Models of Adult Temperament." In *Handbook of Temperament*, edited by Marcel Zentner and Rebecca L. Shiner, 41–66. New York, NY: Guilford Press.

Index

"f" after a locator indicates a figure; "t" after a locator indicates a table

academic performance, improvement through INSIGHTS programme, 111
acceptance of others, 155–56
achievement motivation as a behavioural trait, 11
activity level, 78–81; and attention levels, 79–80; as a behavioural tendency, 14; as a behavioural trait, 11; importance of age and context in assessment of, 79; impulsivity vs motor activity in assessment of, 80–81; as measured by T-SATI, 85t, 86
adaptive parenting, 36
adaptive personality traits, 158
adequate parental responses, 108–9
adopted children, as subject of research, 2, 5, 30
adults, relationships between children and, 159
affectional bond, 23
aggressive behaviour: classroom management practices to reduce, 117; and disoriented attachment pattern, 26; genes associated with, 2, 74; goal of INSIGHTS programme to minimize, 111; in Jamaica, 51, 58, 72; pre-existing levels of and new teachers, 42; resulting from neglect, 34–35; resulting from violent discipline, 53; teacher-child conflicts and prediction of, 39; traced from preschool to school, 45. *See also* bullying
Ainsworth-Salter, Mary D., 23, 29, 36; Strange Situations study, 28, 43–44
Almas, Alisa K., on research regarding regulation of aggression, 74
Alpha Infant School, 147–48; INSIGHTS wall at, 148f
Alumni Engagement Innovation Fund, 91
antagonism as a behavioural trait, 11

approach/sociability, 82–84
aroused infants, 8
Arseneault, Louise, research on bullying, 54
assessment of children's temperament, research on, 9–14
assessment of INSIGHTS intervention in Jamaica, 91, 94–97
attachment: definition of, 30; parent-child relationship, 22–29; parents and peers' connection, 43–44; patterns of, 24–26, 36; and peer relationships, 44; shared features of temperament and, 30; and temperament, 30–32, 36
audio-visual vignettes, use of in INSIGHTS programme: with children, 66, 70; with adults, 64, 67, 109, 112, 136
authoritarian child-rearing style, 33, 37
authoritarian parents, in Jamaica, 51–53
authoritative child-rearing style, 32–33, 34, 37
avoidant attachment pattern, 25, 26, 28, 36

Baker, Jean H., research on teacher-student relationships, 41
Bassett, Hideko Hamada, research on temperamental surgency, 48
Bates, John E., research on self-control, 18
Baumrind, Diana: on categories of child-rearing style, 32–34
beatings, 99, 100. *See also* corporal punishment

behaviour genetics, 14
behaviour: influences on, 2–3; influences of teachers', 48
behaviour management, 93, 118, 135, 143, 155
behavioural problems: control system and, 18; in Jamaican classrooms, 51, 61–62; and parent neglect, 34–35; reduction of with INSIGHTS programme, 71; teacher interaction with, 39
behavioural styles, 20; assessment of, 9–10; changes during maturation process, 8–9
behavioural tendencies, 14
behavioural traits, 11–14
Belsky, Jay, on attachment disorganization, 28, 32
Belsky's process model, 31–32
Bernard van Leer Foundation, 55, 57
Bertoni, Anna Marta Maria, and intervention through Groups for Family Enrichment, 97–98
benign level of environmental stressfulness, 19, 19f
Berk, Laura, 29; on child-rearing styles, 32
biological changes in children, 8
biological families, goodness of fit in, 31
biological relatedness, studies with children having close, 14
biology and temperament, 2
Blandon, Alysia Y., research on temperamental reactivity, 9
bonding patterns of infants, research on, 24t
Bowlby, John, 28

Bronfenbrenner, Urie, ecological theory of, 57
Braungart-Ricker, Julia M., research on avoidant infants, 27
Brown, Janet, research on authoritarian child-rearing style, 52–53
"bully mothers", 99
bullying, 46, 54, 62, 89; adults and, 157
Burke, Taniesha, on Jamaican parenting style, 152

Cappella, Elise, research on efficacy of INSIGHTS programme, 71
caregivers, 4, 9, 20, 23, 26, 90, 106. *See also* mothers; parents; teachers
Carlson, Elizabeth, research on disorganized attachment, 27–28
Caribbean Policy Research Institute, 56
Caspi, Avshalom, on longitudinal study of temperament, 10–11
Cassidy, Jude, on mother-and-peer representation, 43–44
cautious temperament, the Cautious puppet (INSIGHTS) representing, 64f; 66
Centre for Early Childhood Education (CE), Jamaica, 55
challenging temperament, 18
change, temperament seen under conditions of, 5
Change from Within programme, 58–59, 72
changers (in temperament), 9
Chapell, Mark S., on effects of bullying, 46

character. *See* students, character development of
CHASE fund, Jamaica, 91
Chess, Stella, 8, 9, 17; on child temperament and relationship with mother, 31; on goodness of fit, 35
child behaviour-management strategies, 61, 62; different temperaments and, 63
child management, INSIGHTS programme and, 67
child-parent attachments, 43–44
child-rearing styles, 32–36; definition of, 32
child temperament, recognizing and reframing of, 67
childhood development, 157
childhood trauma, 157–58
children, first two years in, 34–35
children's sessions with INSIGHTS programme, 70, 89, 93; understanding classmates' temperaments, 131
chronic stress, 19f, 20
classroom environment, 17, 44–45, 49–50; factors linked to success in, 48–49; quality of, 77–78; restorative justice used in, 58–59; students' and teachers' temperaments impacting, 47–48
Classroom Management (PALS workshop), 60
classroom management practices, 117–19, 131, 143, 147–48
classroom organization, teacher-student interaction as measured by, 77–78
Collins, Ashleigh, on task persistence, 82, 86

Collins, W. Andrew, on influence of parents and peers, 42
communication between parent and child, 109–11, 114–15
compliance, gaining of with INSIGHTS programme, 68–69
compliance as a behavioural trait, 11
confident temperament, 10, 11
conflict management strategies, with INSIGHTS programme, 94
conflict resolution, 58; child employing, 155; in the classroom, 60. *See also* dilemmas
consideration of others as a behavioural trait, 11
contracts: between parent and child, 110–11; between teacher and child, 130, 135–36; and goal-setting, 155
control system, 18
constants (in temperament), 9
Cook, Loraine D., piloting of INSIGHTS programme in Jamaica, 89; rating children's temperament, 85–86; as visiting Fulbright scholar at NYU, 88
Coplan, Robert J., on teacher response to different temperaments, 47, 117–18
corporal punishment, 51–54, 98, 99, 119–20; alternatives to, 90
counterproductive parental responses, 108–9
Creating and Nurturing the School (PALS workshop), 60
Crozier, W.R., on shyness, 75–76
Curby, Timothy W., study on difficult temperament, 77–78

Davies, Rose, piloting of INSIGHTS programme in Jamaica, 89
Deater-Deckard, Kirby, on influence of genetics and environment, 2
Delker, Brianna C., research on poverty and quality of attachment, 26
Demeusy, Elizabeth, on parental neglect and aggression, 35
depression and temperament, 21
Diathesis-Stress Model, 16, 18–20, 21; INSIGHTS programme underpinned by, 62, 156; illustration of central thesis of, 19f
difficult temperament, 5, 31; negative reactivity and shyness as, 77–78
dilemmas: solving of, 45, 61, 63, 70, 93, 96, 136–37, 155; conflicts seen as, 88
discipline, goals of, 119
discipline practices: child-rearing and, 32; INSIGHT programme strategies for, 69; harshness of in Jamaica, 51–53, 119–21, 142, 143, 152, 157; restorative justice as alternative, 58; role of teacher, 127–28
disorganized type, child behavioural trait, 11
disoriented/disorganized attachment pattern, 26, 28, 31, 36
dispute resolution techniques: teaching of through PALS, 59; teaching of through

Managing Conflict and Violence in Schools workshop (PALS), 60
disruptive behaviour: goal of INSIGHTS programme to minimize, 111; longitudinal research on teacher-student relationship and, 39–40
distractibility: as a behavioural tendency, 14; as a behavioural trait, 11
distress: in children, 36; in infants, 7. *See also* stress
Dollar, Jessica M., on anger and development of social skills, 75
dopamine D4 receptor (DRD4), 2, 74
Doumen, Sarah, research on conflict in teacher-student relationships, 40
dysregulation, 74

early childhood: discipline used in, 119; INSIGHTS programme targeting, 91; IY Teacher Training Programme targeting, 61
Early Childhood Commission (ECC), 56, 72, 89–90, 93
early childhood education, 86; teachers in, 38
early intervention, 62
easy temperament, 5, 18
Education Transformation Project (2005), 56
effective parenting, 106
effortful control, 48–49
emotional development, 35, 156, 157
emotional disconnection, 26
emotional individuality, attachment and temperament referring to, 30
emotional support: by teachers, 71; teacher-student interaction as measured by, 77–78
environment, characteristics of, 16–17
environment and temperament, 2, 8, 16–21, 35
environmental effects and behavioural genetics, 15
environmental factors: and interaction with genes, 57; individual's temperament responding to, 20–21
environmental stressfulness, levels of, 19–20
extroverted children. *See* talkative children

facilitators in INSIGHTS programme, 103f, 133, 137
family, importance of, 57
fathers: use of corporal punishment by, 100; role of in child's development, 28–29
Fernald, Lia C.: study on use of corporal punishment in Jamaica, 51, 53, 100, 152; on bullying and peer victimization, 54
first-grade classrooms, INSIGHTS programme efficacy in, 71
Foster, Mrs (principal of Alpha Infant), 150
friendly children, as represented by Fredrico the Friendly puppet, 66, 113
frustration, feelings of: in children, 47, 48, 74, 94, 131,

149; in parents, 100, 107, 156; in teachers, 39, 40, 120, 126, 132

Gallagher, Kathleen, research on temperament and school achievement, 79–81
Garcia, Enrique, on parenting style in Spain, 34
Garcia, Fernando, on parenting style in Spain, 34
genetic mechanism, 14–16
genetics and environment, 2, 18, 57
"getting stuck", 39
Goldsmith, H. Hill, on attachment and temperament, 30
goodness of fit, 16–18, 20, 21, 35, 37; authoritative child-rearing and, 34; child improvement of in classroom context through INSIGHTS programme, 70–71; definition of, 16; INSIGHTS programme underpinned by, 62, 63, 156; parents creating an environment with, 152–54; teachers creating an environment with, 150–52; teachers' interactions and, 46–47
grade 1 teachers, 120–30
Grant, Dudley Ransford Brandyce (DRB), 55
Gregory the Grumpy puppet, 141. *See also* grumpy children
Groups for Family Enrichment, 97–98
grumpy children, as represented by Gregory the Grumpy puppet, 64, 65f, 66, 90, 105, 112–13
Guidelines for Self-awareness (component in INSIGHTS programme), 104

Hamre, Bridget K., on longitudinal research on negativity, 42
hard working children, as represented by Hilary the Hard Worker puppet, 66, 113
Harman, Catherine, on attachment and temperament, 30
Harriott, Anthony D.: on Jamaican children experiencing violence, 51; on parenting style and violence, 100
Hart, Craig H., on authoritative parenting style, 34
Henningham-Baker, H., 54; the IY Teacher Training Programme, 60–61, 72; on role of teachers, 149–50
heritability, 14–15
Herman, Keith C., on negative student-teacher relationships, 40
high activity and achievement, 80. *See also* activity level
high maintenance temperament: Gregory the Grumpy puppet (INSIGHTS) representing, 64, 65f; as substitute term for "problem child", 105
higher-order behavioural tendencies, 13t
high reactive infants, 6, 7, 8
high school teacher-training programmes in Jamaica, 60

high surgency students, 48
hitting. *See* corporal punishment
home environment, 16, 19, 22, 36; relation between environmental stress and behaviour problems mediated by predispositional risk, 19f
How to Structure Responses with high negative reactivity (component in INSIGHTS programme), 104
Howes, Carollee, on teacher-toddler/pre-schooler relationship, 38

Incredible Years (IY) Teacher Training Programme, 60–61, 72
independence, fostering of in children, 69
industrious temperament, Hilary the Hard Worker puppet (INSIGHTS) representing, 64, 65f, 66
infants: and attachment, 36; bonding patterns of, 23; classification of, 5–7
inhibited temperament, 10, 11
inhibition-to-the-unfamiliar: as a behavioural tendency, 14; as a behavioural trait, 11
insecure attachment, 23, 44
insecure/fearful as a behavioural trait, 11
insecurity in infants, 26

INSIGHTS programme in Jamaica, parents' participation in: assessment of, 94–96; frequency of use by parents of information learned from, 101f; helpful components of for parents, 103–4; listening skills, 153–54; new information learned by parents from, 102f; operational structure of, 92–94; Parental Daily Report (PDR), 106; parenting practice influenced by, 97–116; parents' application of principles extending beyond children, 109; parents' descriptors of, 113–14; parents' feedback on, 101–9; parent-rating of facilitators from, 103f; parents' recommendations for, 114–15; parents' reflections on parenting, 98–101; parents' self-awareness, 106–8; parents' use of temperament profiles, 104–6; parents' views on demands of, 112–13; quantitative data for, 94–95; school-based component, 93; self-evaluation by parent, 108–9; social competencies' sessions, 109–11; thinking, forethought, and reasoning taught, 153; usefulness to parents of information from, 102f

INSIGHTS programme in Jamaica, teachers' participation in: amount of information learned from, 122f; application of principles of temperament, 125–27, 142–44; audio-visual vignettes used, 136; and challenges seen, 138–40; changed perception of negative behaviour, 127–28;

contract with parent and child, 130, 135–36, 142; and dependency on school resources, 139–40; effectiveness of facilitator from, 123f; feedback from teachers on, 121–23; frequency of use of information learned from, 122f; homework for, 139; improvement in relationship with parents, 130–33; management of children, 129–30; practices prior to intervention, 119–21; puppets used, 141; responding vs reacting, 129; response strategies, 134; time allocation for, 138–39; understanding of temperament, 124–25; usefulness of information learned from, 123f, 133–36

INSIGHTS into Children's temperament programme, 61–72, 88–96; age of children involved in, 141; effectiveness of, 70–72; findings on the effects of, 156; influence on children, 155–56; intervention curriculum with children, 70; intervention curriculum with parents and teachers, 63–66; key principles of, 67–69; Parental Daily Report (PDR), 106; pilot programme in Jamaica, 89–91; puppets used, 64–65; and school culture, 148; sustainability of principles learned by children, 148–49; sustainability of principles learned by teachers, 146–50

INSIGHTS wall, Alpha School, 148f
instructional support, teacher-student interaction as measured by, 77–78
intelligence as a behavioural trait, 11
intervention programmes, 57, 157. *See also* Change from Within programme; INSIGHTS into Children's temperament programme; Peace and Love in Society (PALS)
irritable temperament, in infants, 36
introverted youth, 82–83

Jamaica: Change from Within programme in, 58–59; child development in, 51–72; corporal punishment, 51–54; criticism by teachers of Ministry of Education, 120; early childhood education in, 55–57; intervention programmes, 57; legislative framework for early childhood education, 55–56; parenting practices in, 52–53, 99–100, 152; Peace and Love in Society (PALS), 59–60; pilot INSIGHTS programme in, 89–91; temperament of children sampled in, 73–87
Jamaican children, survey of temperamental profiles of, 84–86
Jamaican education, crisis in, 56
Jamaican parents, 51–53, 54, 152. *See also* INSIGHTS programme in Jamaica, parents' participation

in Jamaican teachers' assessment of students' temperamental profiles, 84–87
Jennings Craig, Zellyne, piloting of INSIGHTS programme in Jamaica, 89
Jesse Primary School, 147
Johns Gayle, Winsome, piloting of INSIGHTS programme in Jamaica, 89
Johnson, Sharon, research on authoritarian child-rearing style, 52–53
Jones, Ithel, on influence of temperament in teacher-student interactions, 47
Jones, Marlyn, on Jamaican children experiencing violence, 51; on parenting style and violence, 100
Juffer, Femmie, on longitudinal study of temperament, 5, 30–31

Kagan, Jerome, on temperament in newborns, 5–8, 9, 21
Keogh, B., study on teacher-student interactions, 4, 17
Kingston, Jamaica, 91
Koenen, Anne-Katrien, on negative reactivity influencing teacher-student relationships, 75
Kornienko, Dimitry S., on temperament and mother-child relationship, 31
Kotch, Jonathan B., on child neglect, 35
Kuczynski, Leon, on Jamaican parenting style, 152

Lamb, Michael E., research on child interaction with fathers and mothers, 29
Laukkanen, Johanna, on child temperament and mothers' parenting styles, 36
Learning about the Temperament of Children (component in INSIGHTS programme), 104
Lease, Michele, studies of children's behavioural patterns leading to identification of traits, 11
licensing fee, 92
Lipps, Garth, rating children's temperament, 85–86
listening skills, 153–54. *See also* communication between parent and child
longitudinal research on temperament, 21, 27–28, 30–31
low emotional support, 84
low-positivity temperament, 36
low reactive infants, 7; self-reporting by children categorized as, 8
low-self-esteem, 76
low surgency students, 48
Lyons-Ruth, K., on child's aggressive behaviour and parent-child relationship, 27

Main, M., on disoriented/disorganized attachment pattern, 26
Managing Conflict and Violence in Schools (PALS workshop), 59–61
management of children in grade 1, 129–30

Martin, Roy P., studies of children's behavioural patterns leading to identification of traits, 11; on individual temperament responding to environment, 20; temperament theory and INSIGHTS programme, 62

McClowry, Sandee, 4, 16, 18, 83; on activity level, 79; INSIGHTS in Jamaica, 89–90; INSIGHTS into Children's Temperament, 61, 62, 63, 64, 66, 88, 118–19; on task persistence, 82, 86; T-SATI, 85, 87

Meehan, Barbara, on quality of teacher-student relationship, 40

Meeks-Gardner, Julie: study on use of corporal punishment in Jamaica, 51, 53, 100, 152; on bullying and peer victimization, 54

mental health, and problems with resulting from bullying, 54

metacognitive self-awareness, 76

Ministry of Education: Early Childhood Programme (1970s), 55; teacher criticism of, 120

modal or typical level of environmental stressfulness, 19f, 20

Mokrova, Irina, 86; study on role of persistence in math and language skills, 82

molecular genetic studies, 16

mothers, 24; encouragement of aggression in children, 100; and goodness of fit, 35; influence of, 28; parenting style and temperament, 36; and-peer representation, 43–44; psychological control by, 36. *See also* parents

National Parenting Policy (Jamaica), 56

nature and nurture: importance of, 8; influencing negative reactivity, 74

naughty children. *See* negative behaviour

negative affect, 48–49

negative behaviour: early response to, 156; teachers' perceptions changed on, 127–28, 143, 154

negative emotionality as a behavioural trait, 11

negative emotions, 36; in kindergarten, 42; study on teacher-student interactions and, 75

negative emotionality/irritability as a behavioural tendency, 14

negative experiences and "steeling", 158

negative reactivity, 47, 50, 74–75, 100, 144; classified as difficult temperament, 77–78; Gregory the Grumpy puppet, 66; as measured by T-SATI, 85t, 86

neglectful/uninvolved child-rearing style, 33, 34–35, 37

Nelson, K., on negative relationships between students and teachers, 39; research on corporal punishment in Jamaican schools, 53

newborns, tracing temperament from, 5–9
New York University, 88
non-aggressive students, 39
non-compliance of children, 152
non-disruptive students, 39
nurturing environment, 35

O'Connor, E., on improved behaviour with INSIGHTS programme, 106
openness to experience/curiosity as a behavioural trait, 11
optimal parental responses, 108–9
Oren, Meral, on influence of temperament in teacher-student interactions, 47

Palisin, Helen E., on activity level and achievement, 80
Pallini, Susanna, on attachment and peer relations, 44
parent sessions with INSIGHTS programme, 93. *See Also* INSIGHTS programme in Jamaica, parents' participation in
parent-child relationship: and attachment, 22–29, 43–44; and improvements through INSIGHTS programme, 156
parent-teacher collaboration, 154–55
Parental Daily Report (PDR), 106
Parental Responses session (INSIGHTS programme), 107, 153
parenting behaviours, child-rearing styles and, 32
parenting interventions, 97
parenting practice, influenced by INSIGHTS programme, 97–116
parenting stress, 28
parenting styles. *See* child-rearing styles
Parenting Support Commission, 56
parents: behaviour-management skills for, 61, 104; child management skills with INSIGHTS programme, 67–68; child-rearing styles of, 32–37; conjoined with peer influence, 42–43, 50; disciplining of children, 90; fostering social competence in children by, 103–4; frustrations felt by, 100; genetics and environment created by, 2; INSIGHTS curriculum with, 63–66; interaction with their children, 22–37; intervention programmes for, 57, 61; negative experiences with, 45; negative reactivity of, 153; nurturing environment created by, 35; reactions based on children's behaviour, 158; recommendation of INSIGHTS programme, 154; reflections on parenting by, 98–101; responses to children's behaviours and requests, 108–9; self-awareness for, 103, 106–8; self-care for, 69; temperament profiles used by, 104–6. *See also* INSIGHTS programme in Jamaica, parents'

participation in; INSIGHTS into Children's temperament programme
Paris, Joel, on the effects of trauma on children's temperament, 158
Pasco Fearon, R.M., on attachment disorganization, 28
pathological stress level of environmental stressfulness, 19f, 20
Peace and Love in Society (PALS), 59–61, 72
peer experiences: bullying by, 54–55; negative types of, 44, 46; shyness and removal from, 76
peer influence, 42–46; conjoined with parents' influence, 42–43, 50; impact of on parent-child relationship, 43
peer rejection, 76
permissive/indulgent child-rearing style, 33, 34, 37
persistence. *See* task persistence
personality, 3; appreciation of differences in, 61. *See also* temperament
physical abuse, 35. *See also* bullying; violence
Pianta, Robert C., on longitudinal research on negativity, 42
Planalp, Elizabeth M., research on avoidant infants, 27
Plomin, R., on influence of genetics on behaviour, 2
poorness of fit environment, 17
positive emotionality: as a behavioural tendency, 14; as a behavioural trait, 11
Pottinger, A., research on corporal punishment in Jamaican schools, 53
poverty: child-rearing within conditions of, 52–53; bullying and, 54
Prakash, Kavita, on teacher response to different temperaments, 117–18
pre-schoolers, early intervention with, 35
problem behaviours: discouraging of, 34, 62, 143–44; study of preschool to school children and, 45; teacher-student conflicts and, 40; use of contracts with teacher, 130. *See also* INSIGHTS into Children's temperament programme
problem child, 105, 112–13
problem-solving strategies, children learning, 61, 63, 137
Project for Early Childhood Education (PECE), 55
prosocial behaviour as a behavioural tendency, 14
psychological adjustment, 34
psychological control, by mothers, 36
puppets used in INSIGHTS programme, 64–65, 70, 112–13

qualitative data from INSIGHTS programme: results from parents, 115–16; results from teachers, 124–36
quantitative data from INSIGHTS programme: results from parents, 115–16; results from teachers, 121–23
quantitative genetics, 14

reactivity and regulation, 73–74, 83; student success linked to, 48
Read Aloud programme, 119
rejection, sense of, 26
relationships, influences on the quality of, 43–44
Reproductive Health Survey Jamaica (2010), on violence towards children, 52
reserved temperament, 10, 11
resilience, 158
resistant attachment pattern, 25–26, 36
responding vs reacting, teachers, 129
response strategies, teachers', 134
responsibility, fostering of in children, 69
restorative justice, 58–59
Restorative Justice circle, 59
rude behaviour. *See* negative behaviour
Ruiz, Alicia, on violence against young females, 100
Runions, Kevin C., on teacher-child conflicts, 39
Rochat, Philippe, on self-awareness, 76
Roman Catholic educational institution, Alpha School as a, 147
Rose-Krasnor, Linda, on attachment and peer relations, 44
Rothbart, Mary K., 5; research on self-control, 18
Rudasill, Kathleen Moritz, 42; research on temperament and school achievement, 79–81

rural schools in Jamaica, INSIGHTS programme, 94–95

scaffolding, 71, 128, 152
school-based component, INSIGHTS programme, 93
school environment, 19, 38–50; intervention programmes for, 57
school leadership, 146–47
Schneider, Barry Howard, on attachment and peer relations, 44
secure attachment, 23, 44, 158
secure attachment pattern, 24–25, 28, 36
self-acceptance, 155–56
self-awareness, 3, 76; of parents, 106–8; of adults, 159
self-consciousness, 75–76, 157
self-esteem, 34
self-reflection in adults, 159
self-regulation, 73–74
self-regulatory skills, 28, 34
self-talk, 76
Şendil, Çağla Öneren, study on social competence, 83
serotonergic genes, 16
Serrbanescu, Florina, on aggression against female youth, 100
shaming as disciple strategy, 119, 142
Sherlock, Sir Philip, 58
shouting as disciple strategy, 119, 142
shy children, 48, 131; ignored by teachers, 121; represented in Coretta the Cautious puppet, 64, 66, 113; viewed as problem behaviour, 47, 50

shyness, 75–77, 86; classified as difficult temperament, 77–78
Silva, Phil A., on longitudinal study of temperament, 10–11
Slaby, Ron, on adults addressing bullying, 46
Slobodskaya, Helena R., studies of children's behavioural patterns leading to identification of traits, 11
Smiley, Patricia A., on mothers and goodness of fit, 35
sociability, 82–83, 86
social cognition, 3–4
social competence, 44, 83; definition of, 103
Social Competencies for Parents session (INSIGHTS programme), 103–4, 107, 109–11, 153
social development, 35, 156, 157
social/eager to try temperament, Fredrico the Friendly puppet (INSIGHTS) representing, 64, 65f, 113
social-emotional development, 118–19
social interactions, temperament influencing, 20–21
socialization: by parents, 42–43; in school setting, 44–45
social withdrawal as a behavioural trait, 11
Solomon, Judith, on disoriented/disorganized attachment pattern, 26
solution-oriented intervention, 89
Snidman, Nancy, on temperament in newborns, 5–8, 9, 11, 21

Spain, parenting styles in, 34
special education institution, study of teacher-student interactions in, 75
Spellman, Mark, 89, 90
Stams, Geert Jan, on longitudinal study of temperament, 5, 30–31
Stewart, Marcia, piloting of INSIGHTS programme in Jamaica, 89
Storey, Kim, on adults addressing bullying, 46
Strange Situations study, 28, 43–44; summary of episode of the, 24t
"steeling", 158
stress: adaptive personalities against, 158; in environment, 19f, 19–20, 21, 156; in parents, 28, 33; parents activation of in children, 114; in teachers, 114; temperament seen under conditions of, 5. *See also* distress
strong-willed as a behavioural trait, 11
student-teacher relationship, 39, 152. *See also* teacher-student relationship
students: character development of, 152; teacher observations of effects of INSIGHTS programme on, 136–37
substance abuse, problems with resulting from bullying, 54
Suchdev, Danielle, on violence against young females, 100
surgency, 48
surgency-extraversion, 48–49

talkative children, viewed as problem behaviour, 47

task persistence: study on role of in math and language skills, 81–82; as measured by T-SATI, 85t, 86
task persistent temperament, 48–49, 82, 83
teacher-child relationship: conflicts in, 39; and peer relationships, 45; students' problem behaviours relating to, 40
teacher education, in Jamaica, 55
teacher sessions with INSIGHTS programme, 93. *See also* INSIGHTS programme in Jamaica, teachers' participation in
teachers, xii, xv, 16, 45; behaviour-management skills for, 61; burn-out and negative emotions, 75, 117; classroom management practices by, 60, 117–19; collaboration with parents, 154–55; criticism of Ministry of Education, 120; discipline practices in Jamaica, 53; disciplining of children, 90; early childhood, 38; and emotional support for children, 83; and emotional support for children with INSIGHTS programme, 71; expectations for children's behaviour, 120; INSIGHTS curriculum for, 63–66; in Jamaica, xvii; reactions based on children's behaviour; 158; recommendations for INSIGHTS programme from, 140–41; self-care for, 69; temperament of, 17, 47; understanding temperament, 21, 90–91, 124–25; use of negative controls, 40. *See also* INSIGHTS into Children's temperament programme; INSIGHTS programme in Jamaica, teachers participation in
Teacher-School Age Temperament Inventory (T-SATI), 85–86; results of, 85t
teacher-student interactions, study on negativity in, 75; quality of, 77–78
teacher-student relationship, xvi, 38–42, 152; influence of classroom management on, 117–18; influence of INSIGHTS programme on, 156; influence of temperament in, 46–50; restorative justice employed by, 58–59. *See also* teacher-training programmes in Jamaica
teacher-training programmes in Jamaica, 58–63
temperament: and attachment, shared features of, 30; change in during maturation process, 8–9; consideration of, 4–5; definition of, 3–4, 30, 66, 73–74; differences in during early years, 1–3; and environment, 16–20, 156; of Jamaican children sampled, 73–87; longitudinal studies from infancy to adolescence, 7–9, 21; in newborns, 5–7; stability of, 9–14; teacher

response to differences in, 47, 90–91; of teachers, 17, 47; types of, 10–11
temperament theory, 62
temperament profiles: parents use of, 104–6; survey of Jamaican children's, 84–86
temperamental bias, 7
temperamental reactivity, 9
temperamental surgency. *See* surgency
Tharner, Anne, on infant attachment patterns and parenting stress, 28
therapeutic level of environmental stressfulness, 19, 19f
Thomas, Alexander., on child temperament and relationship with mother, 31
time-out strategy, 111
toddlers: teacher's relationship with, 38; teaching social skills to, 75. *See also* children, first two years in
trauma. *See* childhood trauma
Tremblay, Richard E., on child-rearing and discipline, 32; children learning to refrain from physical aggression, 107
twins, studies on, 14

uncontrollable temperament, 10, 11
uniqueness of children, as emphasized in INSIGHTS programme, 70, 89, 96, 155–56
United States Embassy, 91
University of the West Indies, Mona, 58; School of Education, 55, 91, 92

"unshared environment", 158
urban schools in Jamaica, INSIGHTS programme, 94–95

van den Boom, Dymphna C., 30
van Ijzendoorm, Marinus H., on longitudinal study of temperament, 5, 30–31
van Leer, Oscar, 57
verbal abuse, parents using, 99
victims, children as, 46, 51, 53; conflict resolution for, 58
videos. *See* audio-visual vignettes
violence: in Jamaica, 53, 72; parental advice on dealing with, 100
vocabulary, expansion of children's, 137
vulnerability in children, 158
Vygotsky, Lev, on education and importance of environment, 57

Wang, Zhe, on influence of genetics and environment, 2
Webster-Stratton, Carolyn, on negative student-teacher relationships, 40
well-adjusted temperament, 10, 11
White, Jamie, research on temperament and school achievement, 79–81
withdrawal, as measured by T-SATI, 85t
Wong, M., on teacher-child relationship and peers, 45

Printed in the USA
CPSIA information can be obtained
at www.ICGtesting.com
CBHW021512161024
15956CB00001B/56